# NEW DIRECTIONS
# IN PARAPSYCHOLOGY

# New Directions in Parapsychology

*With a postscript by Arthur Koestler*

### Edited by JOHN BELOFF, B.A., Ph.D.
*Department of Psychology, University of Edinburgh*

**The Scarecrow Press, Inc.**
METUCHEN, N.J.

© Paul Elek (Scientific Books) Ltd 1974
First published in Great Britain in 1974
by Paul Elek (Scientific Books) Ltd.

First American edition published 1975 by
The Scarecrow Press, Inc.

ISBN 0-8108-0866-8
Library of Congress Catalog Card No. 75-15489

Printed in Great Britain by
Unwin Brothers Limited,
The Gresham Press,
Old Woking, Surrey

# Contents

# Preface

One advantage of a preface is that it allows one a few last words before one's book finally sees the light of day. Since this book was written, an event has occurred whose repercussions may be so far-reaching that these 'new directions' may soon begin to look more like 'old directions'. I refer to the recent appearance in this country of one, Uri Geller. As of this moment it is not possible to say whether Mr Geller is what he claims to be or whether he is an impostor. We know that he satisfied the scientists who tested him a year ago at the Stanford Research Institute in California. But, though these tests were filmed, no detailed report on them has yet been published and, in any case, however conscientiously the scientists may have done their job, no one can spell out the precise limits of the art of deception. The professional stage illusionists are solidly sceptical of Mr Geller's claims and he, for his part, has so far stubbornly avoided a confrontation with them. Nevertheless, Mr Geller has promised to submit to further tests by accredited scientists in this country and, if he survives them, we shall have to take him very seriously indeed. For, even if one can never *logically* exclude the possibility of trickery, one can, surely reduce its relevance to vanishing-point.

On p. 123, discussing the importance of poltergeist research, I airily remarked on the 'virtual disappearance of physical medium-ship'. Should Mr Geller prove to be authentic, we shall have to reckon in future with a case of physical mediumship the like of which has not been seen since D. D. Home astonished his contemporaries a hundred years ago. Moreover, when D. D. Home arrived here from America in 1855, he set in train a series of events which went far beyond his own immediate phenomena. Soon all over Europe and in every stratum of society, families were engaging in table-turning séances, and Spiritualism as a religious movement swept across the world. After Mr Geller's visit to Britain at the end of 1973, scores of people, but especially children, suddenly discovered that they, too, had the power to bend spoons and forks merely by stroking them. So far these strange powers seem to be as elusive as table-levitations and I know of no case that has yet been properly authenticated, but they are intriguing. Unlike Home, Geller has not yet declared that he has a divine mission—his personal mythology is one that is more in tune with the space-age—and whether he will go on to initiate a new religious movement is not now my concern. But, just as the origins of parapsychology, as a science, can be traced back to the tests which William Crookes carried out on Home between 1870 and 1873, and since these investigations led directly to the founding of the Society for Psychical Research in 1882, so positive research findings on Geller could inaugurate a new era for parapsychology.

Consider the painstaking work of Dr J. G. Pratt as here described in Chapter 5. Parapsychologists from all over the world (including Japan and Tasmania) were eager to make the trip to Prague for the sole privilege of testing Stepanek who, when he was on form, could discriminate clairvoyantly between the white and the green surface of a coloured card in about 55% of trials as against the chance expectation of 50%. Yet the scientific community treated this careful statistical evidence for the reality of ESP with almost total indifference. Now, Geller claims to be able to reproduce drawings presented in sealed-opaque envelopes with a fidelity which requires no statistical evaluation! Already I am finding that my scientific colleagues at Edinburgh who previously paid no attention whatever to parapsychology have suddenly become alerted to the existence of the paranormal.

But, even if the Geller phenomena are genuine, and even if he is willing to submit them to investigation, no science can afford to depend on a single unique individual. Hence, the need for a repeatable experiment is just as pressing as it ever was. Nothing in this book, therefore, would be really superseded. On the contrary the whole field would have received an enormous boost. In particular, the animal work, discussed by John Randall in Chapter 4, would remain as important as ever. Work is already under way on this problem in my own department and our first results have been encouraging. Much the same could be said about the importance of the various other lines of inquiry discussed in these pages, all of which promise to open up new horizons.

The other advantage of a preface is that it enables an editor to thank his contributors, but for whose faithful co-operation there would have been no book. This I am delighted to do herewith but, in particular, I wish to thank Arthur Koestler for his postscript. He firmly declined any form of remuneration so that it was, in fact, an act of pure good-will for the sake of helping a struggling science which he felt had for too long been neglected. His own approach, as can be seen, is not identical with mine. He argues that, between the causal principle on the one side and the operations of pure chance or randomness on the other, there is a third principle in nature waiting to be recognised, and this principle may well underlie much that we here call psi phenomena. As an experimental psychologist I rather hope he is wrong, since an experimenter likes to think that his results are indeed the effects of causes which he has himself manipulated. But whatever differences there may be in our respective points of view—and this is not the place to debate them—I am most grateful for his kindness and for his stimulating comments on this book.

John Beloff
*Dept of Psychology*

January 1974                      *University of Edinburgh*

# Notes on Contributors

BENDER, Hans b. 1907. Freiburg im Breisgau, Germany. Dr Bender holds a Chair of Psychology and Border Areas of Psychology at the University of Freiburg where he is Co-director of the Psychological Institute of Freiburg University as well as Director of the independent *Institut für Grenzgebiete der Psychologie und Psychohygiene* (institute for border areas of psychology and mental hygiene). He also edits the *Zeitschrift für Parapsychologie und Grenzgebiete der Psychologie* to which he has contributed numerous articles. His books include: *Verborgene Wirklichkeit* (hidden reality) 1973; *Telepathie, Hellsehen und Psychokinese* (telepathy, clairvoyance and psychokinesis) 1972; *Unser Sechster Sinn* (our sixth sense) 1971; *Parapsychologie: Entwicklung, Ergebnisse, Probleme* (parapsychology: development, results, problems) 1966 (which he edited); *Parapsychologie* 1953 (revised edition 1970); *Zum Problem der Aussersinlichen Wahrnehmung* (a contribution to the problem of ESP) 1936; *Psychische Automatismen* (psychic automatisms) 1936.

Bender obtained his Ph.D. from Bonn University in 1933 and his M.D. from Strasbourg University in 1942. He has held a number of academic posts in psychology and clinical psychology at the Universities of Bonn and Strasbourg before he took up his present post in 1954. He has established a secure reputation as the foremost parapsychologist of Germany and in 1969 was elected president of the Parapsychological Association. More than most parapsychologists he combines an interest in spontaneous cases with an interest in experimental work.

HONORTON, Charles b. 1946. Deer River, Minnesota, U.S.A. Mr. Honorton is Senior Research Associate at the Division of Parapsychology and Psychophysics, Department of Psychiatry, Maimonides Medical Center, Brooklyn, New York. He is the author of a large number of experimental papers in the Journal of Parapsychology and the Journal of the American SPR and is currently collaborating with T. X. Barber on a book entitled *ESP Revisited* to be published by Aldine-Atherton, New York.

Honorton's career as a parapsychologist began in his under-graduate days at the University of Minnesota where he was research co-ordinator for the Minnesota SPR from 1965–66. He was a Research Fellow at the FRNM Institute for parapsychology from 1966 to 1967 when he moved to his present position. He is on the Board of Trustees of the American SPR and of the Gardner Murphy Research Institute and has served both as secretary and as vice-president of the Parapsychological Association.

Honorton's major research interests include the psycho-physio-logical correlates of psi processes, altered states of consciousness and the development of techniques of psi augmentation.

PRATT, J. Gaither  b. 1910. Winston-Salem, North Carolina, U.S.A. Dr Pratt is on the research staff of the Division of Para-psychology of the Department of Psychiatry of the University of Virginia, Charlottesville, where he holds the rank of Full Pro-fessor. He is the author of: *ESP Research Today:* A Study of Developments in Parapsychology since 1960 (1973); *Parapsycho-logy:* An Insider's view of ESP (1964); and is co-author with J. B. Rhine of *Parapsychology:* Frontier Science of the Mind (1957) and with J. B. Rhine and associates of *Extra-sensory Perception after 60 years* (1940/1966). He is also the author of three monographs and of numerous experimental papers in the parapsychology journals and other scientific periodicals including *Science* and *Nature.*

Pratt studied psychology at Duke University where he obtained his M.A. in 1933 followed by a Ph.D. in 1936 with a thesis on dis-crimination learning in the white rat. But, already in 1932 he had become research assistant to J. B. Rhine in the newly established Duke University Parapsychology Laboratory where he remained until 1963 when it was announced that, with Rhine's retirement from his Chair, the Laboratory would sever its connection with the University and become an independent institute. As one aspect of this transition, Pratt moved to his present post at the University of Virginia. During the early years at the Duke Laboratory his name became associated with such historic experiments as that of the so called 'Pearce-Pratt' series of 1933/34 and that of the 'Pratt-Woodruff' series of 1938/39.

Pratt was among the founders of the Parapsychological Association in 1957 and was its president in 1960. Since then he has been one of its most active officers. He is also on the Board of Trustees of the American SPR. Today Pratt ranks as perhaps the most internationally active of parapsychologists and never hesitates to travel to any corner of the globe whenever anything of parapsychological interest is going on. Besides his frequent visits to Prague during the past decade he has visited the Soviet Union a number of times.

Pratt is first and foremost an experimentalist but the scope of his activities has been as broad as parapsychology itself and one would be hard put to mention any psi phenomenon, from poltergeists to homing pigeons, with which he has not had direct dealings.

RANDALL, John L. b. 1933. Warwick, England. Mr Randall is a biology master at Leamington College, a boys' grammar school. After taking his honours degree in Chemistry with a subsidiary in Biology from Leicester College of Technology he obtained his Graduate Certificate in Education from Leicester University. He then taught for four years at a Secondary Modern School before taking up his present post. He has a long standing interest in parapsychology and has recently helped to introduce a General Studies Course for Sixth Formers which includes philosophical topics and parapsychology. He has also been conducting parapsychological experiments at the school using his pupils as subjects and as helpers. Some of these have been reported in the Journal of the SPR and the Journal of Parapsychology where he has also contributed articles of general and theoretical interest.

Among his many outside interests he lists: youth work, scouting, swimming, yoga and music (he is a church organist). He also studies philosophy and theology and ascribes his motivation as a parapsychologist to the fact that he 'cannot rest satisfied with the mechanist view of life'. While admitting that this disqualifies him as an 'impartial' experimenter (if there is such a thing), he hopes this does not prevent him from trying at all times to be 'an honest and a scientific one'.

RAO, K. Ramakrishna b. 1932. Enikepadu, Krishna District, Andhra Pradesh, India. Dr Rao is Professor and Head of the

Department of Psychology and Parapsychology of Andhra University. He is also Regional President of the Indian Academy of Applied Psychology and Convener of the Parapsychological Society of India. Rao is the author of *Experimental Parapsychology* (1966), a widely used textbook of parapsychology, as well as of *Mystic Awareness* (1972) and *Gandhi and Pragmatism* (1968). He has contributed numerous articles to the parapsychological and other learned journals and has recently co-authored, with P. Sailaja, a monograph *Experimental Studies of the Differential Effect in Life Setting* (Parapsychology Foundation, 1973).

Rao studied both at Andhra University, where he obtained his Ph.D and where he was lecturer in the department of philosophy from 1953 to 1958, and at The University of Chicago where he was Fullbright Scholar and Rockefeller Fellow from 1958 to 1960. He worked at the Duke University Parapsychology Laboratory from 1962 to 1965 when he returned to Andhra University. He was president of the Parapsychological Association for 1965. His career and outlook represent a unique blend of psychology and parapsychology, of Western Science and Eastern Learning.


ROLL, William G. Jr. b. 1926. Bremen, Germany. Mr Roll is director of the Psychical Research Foundation Inc., a private institute set up in 1961 to undertake research on the problem of survival after death. He also edits its quarterly bulletin 'Theta'.

Roll is the author of *The Poltergeist* (1973) and of numerous articles in the parapsychology journals covering a wide variety of topics. Roll graduated from the University of California, Berkeley, in 1949 and obtained a B.Litt from Oxford University in 1960. He was on the staff of the Duke University Parapsychology Laboratory from 1957 to 1960 before taking up his present post which is also in Durham, North Carolina. Roll was one of the founding members of the Parapsychological Association in 1957 and has since repeatedly been elected to its Council on which he has held office a number of times culminating in a term as president in 1964.

Besides being an authority on the survival problem, Roll is well known for his work on poltergeists and has participated in the investigation of a number of such cases. He has also always been interested in the wider philosophical implications of psi and for many years has engaged in theoretical speculations about the nature of psi phenomena. His name has been especially associated with the concept of a quasi-physical 'psi field'.

SCHMIDT, Helmut b. 1928. Danzig, Germany. Dr Schmidt is Research Associate at FRNM Institute for Parapsychology. His experiments using automated testing equipment of his own design have attracted widespread interest on both sides of the Atlantic in recent years. Dr Schmidt came to parapsychology from a background in theoretical physics and quantum theory. After obtaining his Ph.D. from Cologne University in 1954 he has held a number of academic posts in Germany, the United States and Canada. From 1965 to 1969 he was Senior Research Scientist at the Boeing Scientific Research Laboratories at Seattle, Washington State. In 1969 he joined the FRNM Institute and became a full-time parapsychologist and was Director of Research from 1970 to 1972.

# Glossary of Technical and Statistical Terms and Abbreviations used in the Text

**AGENT** In a case of TELEPATHY, the SUBJECT is said to acquire information via another person or *agent*. In a telepathic experiment the agent is often referred to as the 'sender' or 'transmitter' and his task is said to be that of conveying his thoughts to the subject but this is a purely notional conception.

**ALPHA** A characteristic brain-rhythm or brain-wave (see EEG) indicative of a state of pre-sleep drowsiness, relaxation or inattention occurring predominantly in the occipital region of the cortex. It is of low amplitude and has a frequency range of between 8–12 Hz ($=$ cycles per second). Of interest to parapsychologists (see ASC) as a possible index of a psi-favourable condition in the SUBJECT.

**ANALYSIS OF VARIANCE** A statistical technique widely used in experimental psychology which allows the total VARIANCE in a set of data to be broken up into its component variances. In this way it becomes possible to assess the SIGNIFICANCE of the contribution of each of the different variables or sources-of-variation that have entered into the experimental design both independently and in combination with one another (the interaction terms). The relevant test of significance here is the *F* ratio (q.v.). In the parapsychological literature the analysis of variance is still rather rare since it presupposes a somewhat elaborate factorial design of experiment and the uncertainty and delicacy of the psi-effect does not readily lend itself to such a cut-and-dried treatment.

**ASC** Altered States of Consciousness. The expression can be used to cover more or less any mental state other than that of the normal waking condition. The ASCs that are of special interest to parapsychologists include: dreaming, hypnosis, trance states, drug-induced psychedelic states and meditation of the yoga or Zen tradition.

ASPR The American Society for Psychical Research Inc., New York. The Society was originally founded in 1885 largely at the instigation of William James but from 1887 to 1904 it was run as an affiliated branch of the London Society (see SPR) so that in its present form it dates from 1904. It issues a quarterly periodical, The Journal of the ASPR, and, at irregular intervals a volume of Proceedings. Its current Director of Research is Dr Karlis Osis.

BINOMIAL DISTRIBUTION This is the underlying distribution subsumed when testing for the SIGNIFICANCE of a score on any test of the FORCED CHOICE kind which has a fixed *a priori* probability $p$ of a HIT and $q$ of a MISS (where $q = 1 - p$). The distribution is obtained by expanding the expression $(p + q)^n$, where $n$ is the number of trials. In a *bionomial* distribution the mean (or MCE) is always given by '$np$' and the VARIANCE by $npq$. Except in the case where $p = \frac{1}{2} = q$, the distribution is not symmetrical and the degree of skewness will increase as the difference between $p$ and $q$ increases. The distribution is discrete, as in a histogram, with $n + 1$ intervals along the base.

Given a binomial distribution it can be shown that the probability of obtaining *exactly* $x$ hits in $n$ trials is given by the formula: $n!/x!(n-x)! \, p^x q^{n-x}$ where $x$ can take any value from $0 \to n$. Since, however, we are not normally interested in the probability of obtaining a certain *exact* number of hits but rather in the probability of obtaining *not less than* a certain given number of hits, it is necessary to summate the probabilities for each value of $x$ equal to or greater than the given value up to $x = n$. Unfortunately, where $n$ is large this becomes prohibitively tedious without recourse to a computer. Hence, in practice, the assumption is made that the binomial distribution can be taken as approximating to the continuous NORMAL DISTRIBUTION and treating the CR (q.v.) as equivalent to the normal deviate $z$. However, if $p$ is very small (i.e. the event is a rare one) then the so-called *Poisson distribution* rather than the normal distribution should be used as giving the better approximation.

BIOFEEDBACK A recent technique which enables a SUBJECT to monitor ongoing fluctuations in his own physiological processes (e.g. blood-pressure, EEG activity etc.). By use of this technique one can acquire some measure of control over internal processes which would otherwise lie outside the sphere of voluntary influence. The technique has a number of important medical applications but it is of interest to parapsychologists mainly in connection with ASC (q.v.) and with the possibility of controlling the incidence of ALPHA.

BLIND-MATCHING TECHNIQUE A method of testing for CLAIRVOYANCE in which the SUBJECT is required to sort the cards blindly into their respective categories.

CALL In an ESP test using cards the call is the SUBJECT's response or guess.

CHI-SQUARE ($\chi^2$) One of the most widely used tests of SIGNI-FICANCE which is applicable wherever one is dealing with discrete frequency counts as opposed to variable scores. The chi-square value is given by the formula: $\chi^2 = \Sigma(o - e)^2/e$ for all cells where $o =$ the observed frequency per cell and $e =$ the expected frequency per cell. To find the significance of a given chi-square value it is necessary to consult a table of the chi squared distribution which gives the $P$-value (q.v.) for the appropriate DEGREES of FREEDOM. The latter correspond to the number of independent cells involved but, where the data is in matrix form, this becomes: d.f. $= (R - 1)(C - 1)$ where $R$ is the number of rows in the matrix and $C$ the number of columns.

CLAIRVOYANCE A form of ESP in which information is acquired directly from some external source without the mediation of a second mind or person, as opposed to TELEPATHY.

CORRELATION A measure of the degree to which two variables co-vary with one another. Hence correlation coefficient, a value lying between $0 \to 1$ where zero represents complete independence and unity perfect covariation. A negative coefficient implies that the two vary inversely with one another.

The most widely used correlation coefficient is the so-called 'product-moment' coefficient $r$ where $r_{xy} = \Sigma d_x d_y / n \sigma_x \sigma_y$. Thus $r_{xy}$, the correlation between two tests or two variables x and y, is obtained by considering $n$ pairs of scores derived from $n$ subjects tested for both x and y. The scores are here expressed as deviation scores from the respective means for x and y. Thus for each pair of scores there is a cross-product $d_x d_y$ and these cross-products are summated for all $n$ pairs. $\sigma_x$ and $\sigma_y$ are the respective STANDARD DEVIATIONS for the x and y sets of scores.

In dealing with large numbers of tests or variables a *correlation matrix* can be set up where each cell of the matrix represents the $r$ coefficent between a particular pair of tests. *Multiple correlations* can also be computed between a particular variable and a combination of other variables.

CR   Critical Ratio, where CR $= d/\sigma$ (q.v.). This is the most convenient way of expressing the score in a FORCED CHOICE test of ESP or PK. By taking the BINOMIAL DISTRIBUTION involved as approximating to the NORMAL DISTRIBUTION, the CR score can be regarded as equivalent to a normal deviate or $z$ score and the $P$ value obtained by consulting a table of the normal distribution (for greater accuracy it is advisable to deduct $\frac{1}{2}$ from the absolute value of the $d$ score to correct for the discontinuity of the binomial distribution).

Example: On 4 runs using ESP CARDS (open pack) a subject scores 30 hits. Find his CR and $P$ value. Here we have $p = 1/5$, MCE $= np = 100 \times 1/5 = 20$,   $X = 30$,   $d = X - $ MCE $= 30 - 20 = 10$,   $\sigma = \sqrt{(npq)} = \sqrt{(100 \times 1/5 \times 4/5)} = \sqrt{16} = 4$. Hence CR $= d/\sigma = 10/4 = 2 \cdot 5$ (corrected for continuity CR $= 9 \cdot 5/4 = 2 \cdot 375$). From the table of the normal distribution it transpires that for a $z$ deviate of $2 \cdot 37$, the $P$ value (1 tail) $= 0 \cdot 009$. We would not therefore expect to find a deviation above chance as high as this in such a test more than once in 100 replications.

As a general guideline the following table presents a series of CRs with their corresponding $P$ values (1 tail). For the 2 tail situation the $P$ value must be doubled.

| CR | P | CR | P |
|----|-----|----|-----|
| 0·0 | 0·50 | 3·0 | 0·001 |
| 0·5 | 0·31 | 3·5 | 0·0002 |
| 1·0 | 0·16 | 4·0 | $3 \times 10^{-5}$ |
| 1·5 | 0·07 | 4·5 | $3 \cdot 4 \times 10^{-6}$ |
| 2·0 | 0·02 | 5·0 | $2 \cdot 87 \times 10^{-7}$ |
| 2·5 | 0·006 | 5·5 | $1 \cdot 9 \times 10^{-8}$ |

DECLINE EFFECT   Any sequential decline in ESP scoring. This may be either a short-term decline, as within a single RUN or single SESSION, or a long-term decline covering a period of time. It is a typical feature of PSI performance in general.

DEGREES OF FREEDOM (d.f.)   In order to find the $P$ value (q.v.) associated with any particular test of SIGNIFICANCE it is usually necessary to know the relevant *degrees of freedom*. This may be defined as the number of independent units of information making up the quantity in question and is normally equivalent to $n - 1$ where $n$ is the number of units or cases in the sample.

DEVIATION SCORE ($d$)   In a standard ESP or PK test the

deviation score is given by: $d = X - \text{MCE}$, where $X$ is the number of HITS. The $d$ score may be either positive or negative.

DT   Down-Through Technique. A method of testing for CLAIRVOYANCE in which the SUBJECT calls the order of the cards in a shuffled pack *before* any checking takes place.

EEG   Electro-encephalography. A technique for amplifying and recording electrical voltage fluctuations in a living brain using electrodes attached to key positions on the SUBJECT's head. The EEG has proved to be of particular importance in sleep research where various distinctive types of brain-waves or brain-rhythms varying in amplitude and frequency have been identified and related to the successive stages of the sleep cycle. See also ALPHA.

ESP   Extrasensory Perception. The acquiring of information other than through the known sensory channels. PARANORMAL cognition. The two main categories of ESP are (1) TELEPATHY and (2) CLAIRVOYANCE. ESP may be either RETROCOGNITIVE, PRECOGNITIVE or contemporaneous depending on the temporal location of the TARGET.

ESP CARDS   A special pack of cards widely used for ESP tests consisting of 25 cards using the five symbols: star, circle, square, cross and wavy-lines

ESP cards.

In a so-called *closed pack* each symbol is represented exactly five times; in a so-called *open pack* the sequence of symbols is made up on a random basis. A test using ESP cards is typical of a FORCED CHOICE situation. Sometimes referred to as Zener Cards.

$F$   The ratio of the larger to the smaller of two given VARIANCES. Used as a test of SIGNIFICANCE especially in connection with an ANALYSIS OF VARIANCE. The corresponding $P$ value can be obtained by consulting a table of the $F$ distribution under the appropriate DEGREES OF FREEDOM for the respective samples.

FACTOR ANALYSIS   A statistical technique which can be applied to any CORRELATION matrix to determine how many common factors underly the different variables which have been inter-correlated. A gain in economy and intelligibility is achieved if the data can be expressed in terms of the *loadings* of each of the variables on a small number of common factors (the loading is mathematically equivalent to a correlation).

Factor analysis has been used extensively in the sphere of personality assessment where the variables are the trait-scales and the factors correspond to the basic dimensions of personality. Each SUBJECT can be assigned a specific *factor-score* that has been standardised on a sample population, for any given factor, for purposes of comparison.

FORCED CHOICE TEST   ESP test in which the SUBJECT is constrained to select one out of a fixed number of alternatives at each trial. Contrasted with FREE RESPONSE test.

FREE RESPONSE TEST   ESP test in which the SUBJECT is free at each trial to report whatever impressions come to mind. Often pictorial TARGETS are used in this connection. The SIGNIFICANCE of a free response test can be evaluated precisely if an independent judge performs a blind matching of the response-protocols with the set of targets used. Contrasted with FORCED CHOICE.

FRNM   Foundation for Research into the Nature of Man, Durham, N. Carolina. With the retirement of J. B. Rhine from his Chair at Duke University in 1965 the celebrated Duke University Parapsychology Laboratory was terminated and then reconstituted under private auspices as the FRNM Institute for Parapsychology at premises outside the campus. Its official organ is the Journal of Parapsychology and its current Director of Research is W. J. Levy.

GESP   General ESP = either TELEPATHY *or* CLAIRVOYANCE. The term telepathy is now rarely used in experimental parapsychology on account of the difficulty of excluding clairvoyance. Hence the more non-commital technical term GESP.

HIT   In a standard test of ESP or PK a HIT is scored whenever the response on any trial matches the TARGET. A response that is not a hit is a MISS.

MCE   Mean Chance Expectation. This is the theoretical score that would be expected in an ESP or PK test on the NULL ASSUMPTION that nothing apart from chance factors were operating. In a FORCED CHOICE test of $n$ trials with a fixed probability of a HIT per trial of $p$, MCE = $np$.

**MISS**   Any response which is not a HIT is a MISS. If, in a FORCED-CHOICE situation, $p =$ the probability of a hit, then $q =$ the probability of a miss where $q = 1 - p$.

*n*   Number of trials in a given test or number of cases or scores in a given sample. Where several samples are involved these can be denoted by means of subscripts: $n_1$, $n_2$, etc.

**NORMAL DISTRIBUTION**   This is the underlying distribution that is assumed when applying most so-called parametric tests of significance and statistical measures (see *F*, *t*, CR, *r*, etc.). It is a mathematical function that takes the familiar bell shape where the vertical ordinate represents frequency and the horizontal ordinate deviation from the mean or norm. In a normal distribution the VARIANCE is, by convention, taken as unity and thus the theoretical STANDARD DEVIATION is likewise unity and the *z* value or normal deviate is the distance in standard deviations from the mean which, again by convention, is taken as zero.

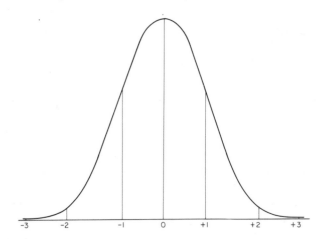

Normal distribution.

It can be shown that any variable which depends on a large number of independent parameters that are additive in combination will tend to be normally distributed in a random sample. This is exemplified by such polygenic variables as height or IQ in a human population. This applies also to the case of measurement where any particular observation may be thought of as combining the true measure with some random experimental error displacing it in one or the other direction, hence the normal distribution is also known as the 'Gaussian' *Curve of Error*.

The normal distribution can be regarded as the ultimate development of the BINOMIAL DISTRIBUTION $(p + q)^n$ where $n$ tends towards infinity, the intervals along the base become infinitesimal and $p = \frac{1}{2} = q$.

NULL ASSUMPTION   Before it is possible to draw any valid conclusion from the result of an experiment it is first necessary to consider the null assumption, i.e. that the results might be explained as due to chance factors alone. If it can be shown that such an assumption is very improbable (see $P$) only then are we entitled to consider the specific hypothesis on which the experiment was predicated.

OBE   Out-of-Body Experience. The experience of seeing the world including one's own body from an external vantage point in space and, sometimes, of travelling through space in a disembodied fashion. An hallucination of high verisimilitude of special interest to parapsychologists on account of its supposed connection with CLAIRVOYANCE. It is also of interest to students of the idea of survival as providing a living example of what disembodied existence could be like. It figures in the older literature under such names as 'astral projection' or 'travelling clairvoyance'.

$P$   Given the outcome of some test, the $P$ value tells us what is the probability of an outcome as deviant or more deviant than the one we have obtained on the NULL ASSUMPTION. If the $P$ value is less than $0\cdot01$ it is usual to reject the null assumption and to consider the result SIGNIFICANT. The $P$ value is obtained by considering what proportion of the relevant distribution of scores lies *beyond* a given deviation from the mean. The $P$ value may be either 1 tail or 2 tail. If we predict in advance that the deviation will lie in a particular direction, say in the above-chance region, and agree to ignore any result no matter how deviant that lies in the opposite direction, then we are entitled to apply the 1 tail test. Otherwise we must use the 2 tail test. For a deviation of given absolute value $P_{(2\ tail)} = 2P_{(1\ tail)}$.

Example: $P_{(1\ tail)} = 3 \times 10^{-5}$ would mean that we would not expect to find a deviation from MCE in the predicted direction as great or greater than this more than 3 times in 100 000 replications of the test, given the NULL ASSUMPTION that the result is due to chance alone.

$p$   In a standard ESP or PK test, the $p$ value is the *a priori* probability of making a HIT on a given trial. Thus, if there are *a* alternative TARGETS and each has an equal probability of occurring at any given trial, $p = 1/a$.

Examples: with ESP CARDS, using a *closed pack*, $p = 1/5$. In a binary PK task, e.g. trying to influence the fall of a coin, $p = 1/2$.

PA Parapsychological Association (no fixed headquarters). Founded in 1957, it remains the only professional organisation of parapsychologists with a select membership of around two hundred active members. It is international in composition but predominantly American. The Council is elected annually and so is the president. It publishes proceedings of its annual conference.

PARANORMAL A phenomenon is said to be *para*normal if in one or more respects it exceeds the limits of what, on current scientific assumptions, is deemed to be physically possible. It has much the same connotations as the word 'miraculous' though not, of course, the same religious overtones.

PARAPSYCHOLOGY The scientific study of paranormal and, more especially, of PSI phenomena (e.g. ESP, PK). It has come to supersede the older expression 'psychical research'. Hence also parapsychologist, parapsychological etc.

PF Parapsychology Foundation Inc., New York. A private organisation founded in 1951 to promote the study of parapsychology throughout the world by subsidising research, organising annual conferences and publishing books, monographs and proceedings. From 1959 to 1968 it also issued the International Journal of Parapsychology. Mrs Eileen Garrett was president until her death in 1970 when she was succeeded by her daughter Mrs Eileen Coly.

PK Psychokinesis. PARANORMAL action. In a PK test the SUBJECT is required to influence some prescribed physical object or process, the TARGET, by means other than the use of the known muscular effectors. A non-mechanical 'mind over matter' effect.

POLTERGEIST A spontaneous outbreak of assorted paranormal physical phenomena of a peculiarly bizarre character centring on a person, known technically as the POLTERGEIST FOCUS and lasting usually for a period of some months. Sometimes referred to in the technical literature as RSPK (Recurrent Spontaneous PK). From the German, lit. 'noisy spirit'.

POLTERGEIST FOCUS The putative SUBJECT of a POLTERGEIST outbreak, usually a child or adolescent.

POLYGRAPH   Apparatus for recording the fluctuations of some physiological variable such as rate of respiration or EEG activity. It consists of electronically operated pens which leave a trace on a band of paper passing across them at a constant speed. Of special relevance to the study of ASC.

PRECOGNITION   A form of ESP in which information is supposed to be acquired directly from some future source. Hence *precognitive.* Cf. RETROCOGNITION.

PRF Psychical Research Foundation Inc., Durham, North Carolina. A private organisation founded in 1961 by Charles Ozanne to promote the scientific study of the question of an afterlife. Its Director is W. G. Roll who is also editor of its quarterly bulletin 'Theta'.

PSI  PARANORMAL phenomena conceived as mind-dependent, i.e. as critically dependent on a human or animal SUBJECT. The Two main categories of PSI are:

(1)  ESP or paranormal cognition and
(2)  PK or paranormal action.

The term is used in various compounds e.g. psi ability, psi factor, psi process, psi effect etc. From Greek letter $\psi$, as in $\psi v \chi \acute{\eta}$, psyche = soul.

PSI HITTING   Scoring in a test of ESP or PK that is consistently and significantly *above* MCE. Hence *psi hitter*, one who exhibits this tendency. Cf. PSI MISSING.

PSI MISSING   Scoring in a test of ESP or PK that is consistently and significantly *below* MCE. Hence *psi misser,* one who exhibits this tendency. Cf. PSI HITTING.

PUNCH TAPE   Tape on which the trial by trial target-response sequence can be automatically registered and can then be fed directly into a computer for analysis. Used in automated tests of ESP or PK.

RETROCOGNITION   A form of ESP in which information is supposed to be acquired from sources in the past. Hence *Retrocognitive.* Cf. PRECOGNITION.

RNG Random Number Generator. Electronic apparatus incorporating a randomising element capable of generating a random sequence of outputs. Used in automated tests of ESP or PK for generating target sequences. A *binary* RNG has two equiprobable outputs.

RSPK   Recurrent Spontaneous PK. A term recently introduced by W. G. Roll to designate POLTERGEIST phenomena.

RUN   A fixed group of TRIALS into which the SESSION is subdivided for purposes of analysis. Usually there is a pause between each run. In a standard ESP test using ESP CARDS the length of the run is 25 trials corresponding to the size of the standard pack. *Mean run score* = average number of hits per run.

SESSION   The series of trials completed on a single occasion or sitting.

SHEEP–GOAT HYPOTHESIS   As originally put forward by Gertrude Schmeidler it states that those who believe in the reality of ESP (sheep) will tend to score *above* chance while those who disbelieve or doubt the reality of ESP (goats) will tend to score *below* chance. The expression 'super-sheep' or 'white sheep' is sometimes used for those who not only believe in ESP but believe that they possess this ability.

SIGNIFICANCE   The improbability of a given result on the NULL ASSUMPTION. Hence, *test of significance*. The *lower* the P value associated with a given score, the *greater* its significance. Alternatively, significance may be expressed as odds-against-chance where the odds correspond to the reciprocal of the P value. In that case the *higher* the odds the *more* significant the result.

SPR   Society for Psychical Research, London. The parent body of all subsequent learned societies whose aim is to promote the impartial study of the evidence for paranormal phenomena. It was founded in 1882 with the philosopher, Henry Sidgwick, as its first president. It has an elected membership and an elected council who, in turn, annually appoint a president. Since 1882 it has issued volumes of Proceedings, at irregular intervals, and, since 1884, the quarterly Journal of the SPR.

STACKING EFFECT   A spuriously high (or low) score in an ESP test which may arise when a large number of SUBJECTS have to guess against a common TARGET sequence. It is due to a fortuitous relationship occurring between the guessing bias of the subject population and the peculiarities of the target sequence and thus cannot be taken as indicative of ESP. Various statistical corrections are used to discount the stacking effect.

STANDARD DEVIATION (SD)   The square root of the VARI-

ANCE. A measure of scatter widely used in tests of SIGNI-FICANCE and for standardising raw scores.

For the BINOMIAL DISTRIBUTION, the theoretical standard deviation *sigma* ($\sigma$) is given by the formula: $\sigma = \sqrt{(npq)}$    **q.v.**

SUBJECT  In psychology or parapsychology the subject is the person (or animal) being investigated whose responses furnish the data of the test or experiment.

*t*  The *t* value represents the ratio of the difference between the means of two sets of scores over the combined standard error (*see* SD) of those means (for the complete formula see any standard textbook of statistics). It can thus be used as a test of SIGNIFICANCE for comparing the difference between two independent samples e.g. a control group and an experimental group. The corresponding *P* value (q.v.) for a given *t* value can be found by consulting a table of the *t* distribution under the appropriate DEGREES OF FREEDOM.

TARGET  In an ESP experiment the target is the 'extrasensory stimulus' i.e. the object, symbol, event etc. which the SUBJECT has to guess or ascertain. In a PK experiment the target is the prescribed outcome which the subject has to try mentally to attain or bring about. Hence *target sequence*.

TC  Transpersonal Consciousness. A type of ASC in which awareness of the self is lost in an awareness of the world at large or of other beings. It is said to typify certain mystical states which can be induced by meditation.

TELEPATHY  A form of ESP in which the SUBJECT is said to acquire information about the TARGET from another person, the AGENT, who has normal knowledge of it. Contrasted with CLAIRVOYANCE. See also GESP.

THETA  A recent term introduced by W. G. Roll to denote whatever it is that is supposed to survive in a case of post-mortem survival. From Greek letter $\theta$, Theta, as in θάνατος, thanatos = death.

TRIAL  The unit of performance in a psychological or para-psychological test. For each trial the SUBJECT is assigned a certain score.

U CURVE  A scoring trend that shows an initial drop in scoring followed by a recovery. Likewise an *inverted* U curve, where an initial rise in scoring is followed by a decline.

VARIANCE (*V*)   The mean squared-deviation i.e.

$$V = \Sigma\, d^2/n \qquad\qquad \text{q.v.}$$

This is the basic measure of scatter for all parametric statistics. It has the useful property of being additive so that if *V* is the variance of a sample of size *n*, 2*V* will be the variance of a sample of size 2*n*. In the case of the BINOMIAL DISTRIBUTION the theoretical variance, $\sigma^2$, is given by the formula:

$$\sigma^2 = npq \qquad\qquad \text{q.v.}$$

See also ANALYSIS OF VARIANCE.

# Introduction

**JOHN BELOFF**

## BASIC CONCEPTS AND METHODOLOGICAL OPTIONS

Parapsychology means the scientific study of the 'paranormal', that is, of phenomena which in one or more respects conflict with accepted scientific opinion as to what is physically possible. The class of paranormal phenomena which mainly interests the parapsychologist is that which critically involves a human or animal subject, the presumption being that mind is somehow instrumental in accomplishing what would otherwise be impossible. Such phenomena are variously referred to as 'parapsychological', 'parapsychical', 'psychical' or 'psychic' but throughout this book we shall follow the convention now widely current in the technical literature and use the abbreviation 'psi'.

Psi phenomena fall into two main categories: psi cognition, better known as ESP (Extrasensory Perception), and psi action, better known as PK (Psychokinesis). Psi cognition or ESP can further be subdivided according to whether it is presumed to depend on another person (the 'agent') whose normal cognitive processes constitute the source of the information, in which case it is referred to as 'telepathy', or whether it is presumed to be independent of any such mediation so that the information comes directly from the target object or event, in which case it is referred to as 'clairvoyance'. If, in addition, ESP is presumed to operate independently of the physical parameters of space and time the target can, in theory, be located either in the past, the present or the future so that psi cognition can be either retrocognitive, contemporaneous or precognitive as the case may be. This allows for a sixfold classification of the varieties of ESP as shown in Table I.1.

The classification given in Table I.1, however, must be regarded as largely academic for, as soon as one begins to consider the practical problems involved in demonstrating one specific type of ESP it is by no means clear how one can be sure that this type alone is operative to the exclusion of all others. In particular it is

TABLE I.1   Varieties of ESP

| Presumed Condition for Success | Presumed Location of Target | | |
|---|---|---|---|
| | Past | Present | Future |
| Agent necessary | Retrocognitive Telepathy | Contemporaneous Telepathy | Precognitive Telepathy |
| Agent not necessary | Retrocognitive Clairvoyance | Contemporaneous Clairvoyance | Precognitive Clairvoyance |

virtually impossible to demonstrate unequivocally the existence of 'pure telepathy' since, at some point in the procedure, it becomes necessary to introduce some physical target and this could, in theory, become known by some variety of clairvoyance. Moreover, even without a physical target, the agent's thoughts will be accompanied by certain physical processes in his brain and this, again in theory, could provide the target for clairvoyance. For technical purposes, therefore, the popular term 'telepathy' is generally avoided in favour of the more noncommittal term 'GESP' (General ESP) meaning 'either telepathy or clairvoyance'. This is, however, a somewhat pedantic usage and, if the design of the experiment is such that the role of the agent is taken as critical there is no harm in describing it as a telepathic design of experiment. Note that there is no similar difficulty about demonstrating 'pure clairvoyance' since, if the test is scored by machine, and only the overall score is recorded, no other *person* need ever know which was the correct target for any given trial.

The varieties of PK are less easy to enumerate. Distinctions are drawn, however, according to the nature of the target, whether it is animate or inanimate or whether it is micro or macroscopic. The influence of mental events on plant growth or on the regeneration of animal tissues would be examples of PK involving animate targets, similarly, a mental influence on the emission of an electron from a radioactive source would represent a case of PK with a microscopic target. We cannot always be certain, however, whether we are dealing with PK or with ESP. When, for example, the subject is asked to predict the outcome of some random process does he rely on his precognitive ESP or does he try to influence the randomiser by means of PK? Similarly, when the agent is trying to transmit information by telepathy, might he not simply be influencing the subject's motor response by PK, especially if the subject happens to be an animal? It is not so difficult, however, to exclude ESP as an explanation of a PK effect for, in the standard PK experiment, the subject is told in advance what is to count as the correct target and success can therefore be attained only by some kind of 'willing' rather than by guessing.

In present circumstances, however, it matters very little whether we can specify the precise relationship which holds between telepathy and clairvoyance or between ESP and PK. What matters, what alone is crucial for the survival of parapsychology as a distinctive science, is whether communication of some kind between the individual and his environment is possible by means other than those of the known sensorimotor channels. To go further, at this stage, and to attempt to codify an elaborate taxonomy of psi processes is to indulge in a sterile scholasticism. It is only in relation to the standard methodological paradigms of psi testing that the kind of distinctions we have been discussing become important. Thus, if we consider the typical guessing situation, where the subject guesses against a random sequence of alternative targets, then, so long as he registers his guess *before* the target for that trial is chosen, this is, by definition, a test of precognition. If the subject registers his guess *after* the target has been selected but before anyone else yet knows what it is, this qualifies as a test of clairvoyance. Finally, if the subject registers his guess *after* the target has been selected *and* after someone else knows what it is, then you have a so called GESP test.

The typical psi test, whether of guessing or of willing, relies on a 'forced choice' procedure, that is the possible responses which the subject can make are laid down beforehand. An alternative procedure which we shall also encounter in the course of this book is the 'free response' test. Here the subject is under no such constraints. He may, for example, know in general the designation of the target which he has to ascertain by ESP, that it is a picture, an object, a person, an inscription, an emotional state etc., but he is free to report whatever impressions come to mind which he thinks may be relevant. Such a test can be scored only by the expedient of using a judge who does not know which target was used for which trial and so in matching a given response with a given target must depend on the degree of resemblance which he can discern between the two. Although any particular judgment he makes will to some extent be subjective, the matching which he eventually produces can be evaluated in strict quantitative terms and the exact probability of its being due to chance can be calculated just as if it were a forced choice test.

The use of the free response procedure has enabled experimental parapsychologists to broaden their repertoire. For there are various situations where a forced choice procedure simply would not be practicable and there are grounds for thinking that it is just such situations that are likely to be most conducive to the operations of psi. I have in mind especially the so called altered states of consciousness, hypnosis, dreams, trances, drug intoxication etc. which do not lend themselves to repetitive decision making but which are richly productive of spontaneous imagery. Provided a protocol can be obtained from the subject during or immediately following one such state an appropriate matching procedure can be carried out and the test duly evaluated. This approach is illustrated with a wealth of examples by Honorton in Chapter 2.

Another distinction of which we must take note is that between the spontaneous psi phenomena of real life and the controlled phenomena of the laboratory. The former, inasmuch as they are spontaneous, cannot be investigated experimentally, at most they can be accurately observed and recorded. And since the present volume is concerned predominantly with parapsychology as an experimental science the emphasis will be overwhelmingly on phenomena of the latter sort. Nevertheless, we must remember that each of the classic types of psi phenomena which we have been considering has its counterpart in real life where it was already familiar long before the possibility of an experimental parapsychology was envisaged. Moreover, the intrinsic interest and dramatic qualities of spontaneous psi and the relative abundance of the data so far exceed anything that can be found in the laboratory that many parapsychologists still consider it amply worth their while to devote themselves to the study of such cases in spite of the well known difficulties and hazards involved in establishing their authenticity. They hope, moreover, that from the careful sifting and collating of innumerable spontaneous cases certain patterns and relationships may emerge which might then suggest hypotheses suitable for experimental testing.

One striking example of a psi phenomenon for which there is a plethora of evidence spanning many centuries and many different countries is that of the so called 'poltergeist'. This clearly belongs to the category of PK since it involves physical disturbances and movements of objects of a paranormal nature. W. G. Roll, an authority on this phenomenon, has suggested elsewhere that the noncommital expression 'RSPK' (Recurrent Spontaneous PK) be used in this connection. However, in questions of nomenclature it is difficult to dislodge a term that has already gained wide currency and it is unlikely that the familiar word 'poltergeist' (German for noisy spirit) will be superseded. Although the spasmodic and unpredictable incidents of a poltergeist outbreak makes them frustrating as objects of study, the remarkable persistence with which such outbreaks go on recurring at odd intervals and in odd places and the many common features they reveal both with regard to the physical manifestations and with regard to the personality of the poltergeist 'focus' (i.e. the person around whom the disturbances appear to revolve) insures for them an important place in the parapsychological literature. For, even though many reported cases can be dismissed as due to trickery or to natural causes like subterranean water courses, a hard core of puzzling evidence remains. In Chapter 6, Hans Bender discusses a number of recent cases in Germany with which he has been associated where the instrumental aids and resources of modern technology were brought in to supplement naked observation.

Within the experimental field, two well tried alternative strategies are available: the one consists of an intensive investigation of a particular individual thought to have some special psi ability, the other consists of the extensive investigation of large numbers of unselected volunteers. Both strategies have their respective advantages and disadvantages and both will be illustrated in the chapters which follow. An excellent contemporary example of the former is J. G. Pratt's massive longitudinal study of the Czech guessing subject Stepanek (see Chapter 5). There was a time when investigators were almost exclusively preoccupied with the special subject who, as often as not, was someone of mediumistic pretensions. But today the balance has shifted decisively in favour of group testing and the contents of this volume reflects this bias. There are several reasons why this should be the case. First there is the harsh fact that good subjects have become increasingly hard to find. In former times, it is doubtful whether someone whose repertoire was as limited as Stepanek's and whose scoring rate was as mediocre would have been thought worth prolonged investigation but today parapsychologists are prepared to journey half way round the world for the privilege of testing him. Secondly, the desire to bring parapsychology closer in line with general psychology and more especially with personality theory makes it necessary to compare large groups of subjects differing on some relevant psychological dimension. And, thirdly, it seemed to many parapsychologists and, notably to J. B. Rhine, implausible to suppose that psi abilities should be present only in certain favoured members of the human species and wholly absent in all others. The work of K. R. Rao (see Chapter 3) using children as subjects, gives support to this assumption of psi as a function of mind in general.

The recent incursion of parapsychology into the field of animal experimentation represents, perhaps, the ultimate development of a methodology freed from dependence on the special subject. In view of the dominating role of the animal subject in modern experimental psychology, especially in modern learning theory, it may seem surprising that it has taken parapsychology so long to follow suit. No doubt this had something to do with the fact that the use of animals was closely bound up with the behaviouristic approach in psychology against which parapsychology was in revolt. Yet folklore had always credited animals with psychic powers of various kinds even if the animals in question were usually dogs or cats or horses, animals which consort with man and to some extent share his concerns, and their psychic powers were subservient to their masters. The idea that rodents, insects or other lowly organisms might possess autonomous psi abilities comparable with those of a human guessing subject provoked a marked revulsion in some quarters as if this somehow detracted from the dignity of psi as a special attribute of the human soul. However, in the light of the findings discussed by John Randall in Chapter 4, where he describes recent automated experiments using small mammals and other work of this kind, it looks as if we shall have to start thinking of psi as a universal property of animal life. Certainly those who still cling to the idea that the 'an-psi' (animal psi) findings may be explainable as indirect manifestations of the psi processes of the human experimenter will find little support in the evidence Randall presents. From a methodological standpoint this new direction which parapsychology has taken should be gratifying. The notorious elusiveness of psi was at least partly a consequence of its dependence on such temperamental individualistic and unpredictable subjects as human beings. Animals, especially laboratory bred animals, are relatively homogeneous and, even if, by good fortune, one were to find a particular individual animal that showed an extraordinary aptitude for psi tests there should be no special problem about breeding a colony or strain of such animals if such an aptitude proved to be genetic.

There is one final problem which calls for mention in this introduction, the problem of postmortem survival. The critical question here is whether psi communication of any sort can take place between a living human subject and the discarnate mind of a deceased person. This, of course, was the problem which above all others preoccupied the founders of psychical research in the 19th century and to men like Fredric Myers or Oliver Lodge, deeply imbued as they were with spiritist beliefs, there was no more important question to which the new science could address itself. But time brings changes and today many parapsychologists are embarrassed by this legacy. It may seem strange, therefore, that we have seen fit to include it in a book devoted to 'new directions'. Yet the problem refuses to go away and, in recent years, has even begun to show fresh signs of vigour. The scholarly and extensive investigations of Ian Stevenson on cases of the reincarnationist type is an illustration of this point. But, quite apart from its intrinsic interest, the problem poses some of the most challenging and sophisticated questions that confront the parapsychologist. For example, given the varieties of ESP that we set out in Table I.1 and given the fact that their limits and scope are unknown, how, in principle, are we to tease out the contribution of the surviving entity, if any such exists, to a given mediumistic communication from that of the medium herself? Some have argued that, until we know more about ESP the problem is insuperable but, even if we cannot reach any definite conclusion, this does not mean that we cannot discuss the relative plausibility of one interpretation of the evidence as against another. In Chapter 7, W. G. Roll puts forward the interesting suggestion that, in the meanwhile, the problem may be tackled from the other end, as it were, that is we could try examining the living subject for evidence of some form of mental activity that is not dependent on the physical organism or on the nervous system and so could conceivably survive their death and dissolution. He believes that some such indications are already forthcoming from the study of 'out of body' experiences and of states of what he calls 'transpersonal' consciousness. Be that as it may, it seems likely that, for a long time to come, the question of what happens to us when we die, whether we continue to exist in any form, will intrigue and baffle inquirers as it has done ever since Socrates debated the question with his disciples.

## THE CURRENT STATUS OF PARAPSYCHOLOGY

Despite the widespread public interest which the topic has always aroused it must be admitted that parapsychology has developed in relative isolation from the mainstream of modern science and philosophy and has so far had little influence on the directions it has taken. An historian of ideas, writing about the

20th century could readily be excused if he omitted to mention it altogether. Progress has been so slow and uncertain, setbacks and false dawns so frequent, that outsiders have naturally been reluctant to commit themselves on matters about which even the experts disagreed. It is noteworthy that such intellectual giants of the past generation as Bertrand Russell or Karl Popper, to name but two who cannot be accused of any narrowness of interest or outlook, were quite content to think and write as if the paranormal was not something which a rational man need take into consideration. The fact that an enormous number of careful observations on this question had been amassed over the previous century counted for nothing. So far as they were concerned nothing had changed in this respect since the 18th century when Hume wrote his famous essay on miracles. The evidence was never quite conspicuous enough to offset the suspicion which invariably surrounded it. The more salient claims could always be put down to trickery while the marginal ones were dismissed as experimental error.

And yet, if the parapsychological evidence is valid, it would, I think, be no exaggeration to say that nothing in science or philosophy could ever again be quite the same. For one thing we should have to acknowledge that our ignorance about ourselves and about the universe we inhabit is far more extensive than we had been led to suppose given the current scientific world picture. Nor is it any escape to point to the extreme marginality of such psi effects as have been demonstrated. Small anomalies in science may have far reaching implications and phenomena trivial in themselves may sometimes overturn long established assumptions. The extreme lengths to which critics of parapsychology are prepared to go to discredit the evidence, which do not stop short of impugning the honesty of the experimenters, testify to its subversiveness and draws attention to how much is at stake. If, then, the reality of psi could be established beyond all reasonable doubt so that no educated person could any longer afford to overlook the fact, the influential thinkers of the next generation would be forced to come to terms with it whatever the consequences.

Some of the contributors to this volume would say that this point has already been reached. That there is no longer any excuse for anyone, who is sufficiently numerate to understand the meaning of statistical significance, to doubt the authenticity of the sort of evidence to be found within these covers. Only those whose minds are made up in advance can still remain unconvinced. Certainly if one turns to Table 4.1, Chapter 4, for example, one would be hard put to escape from this conclusion. And yet such a conclusion would, I believe, be premature. It rests upon a too simplistic and too impatient view of how recognition in science is attained. It ignores, in the first place, the ubiquitous 'factor X' to which not even the most carefully planned experiment is immune. I allude here to the unknown hypothetical variable which the experimenter neglects to control for (he can after all only take account of a finite number of variables) but which, for ought that we know to the contrary, was responsible for the critical effects. Science in its time has witnessed so many spurious claims that fail to live up to a brilliant initial promise—one need only think of the medical field in this connection—that the possibility of a given claim being based on an artefact can be ignored only at its peril. Clearly, something more is required than competent and well intentioned experimenters or statistically impeccable results.

What that something amounts to I shall now try and make clear. Before any claim, great or small, can be accepted definitively as a fact at least one or other of the following conditions must be met. Either we must be in a position to explain the phenomenon in question to an extent where we can predict when it should and when it should not occur or, failing any such theoretical understanding, we need overwhelming inductive grounds for believing that such and such procedures can be relied upon to produce such and such effects even though no one can say why this should be so. Only then can the particular observations and experiments upon which the claim is founded cease to have more than an historic interest and disputes about the honesty or competence of experimenters cease to be relevant. For, at that point, it is open to any critic or doubter to try replicating the findings for himself.

Now there seems little likelihood of the first of our two conditions being met within the foreseeable future. Not that parapsychologists have ever been averse to theorising but their efforts have never gone much beyond a very general speculative or metaphysical level that has had little bearing on the conduct of research. The idea beloved of the science fiction enthusiast that we are on the brink of a scientific revolution after which everything will become intelligible and psi phenomena will lose the stigma of their paranormality and be accepted as no less natural than any other kind of psychological phenomenon can be dismissed as so much wishful thinking. It is a prospect for the next millennium, not for the next decade. On the other hand, with regard to the second of our two conditions, there is nothing very utopian in the suggestion that parapsychology is already edging its way towards a solution of the problem of repeatability. The ensuing chapters, especially Chapter 4, will, I think, bear me out.

It is possible, of course, that I have misread the signs. Some parapsychologists argue forcibly that the inherent instability and elusiveness of psi, the fact that it is not under the subject's conscious control, makes any talk of strict repeatability vain. Given sufficient ingenuity and inventiveness, however, science has in the past managed to cope with even the most elusive of entities—consider what was involved in establishing the existence of neutrinos! At any rate with so much at stake the goal is certainly worth pursuing and in view of the progress already made it would be defeatist to abandon it at this juncture. The most important of the new directions in parapsychology, in my view, are precisely those that bring it closer to this end. Accordingly, the accent of this book is on the concrete and painstaking empirical research that is going on and away from speculations and academic controversies.

Already evidence of the calibre and quality here displayed is beginning to have an effect on the academic, scientific and medical establishments in making for a more tolerant attitude. For example, in December 1969, the Parapsychological Association (the one professional organisation in this field) was admitted to affiliation with the AAAS (American Association for the Advancement of Science). Many more universities and colleges, especially in the United States, now include courses on parapsychology. The latest editions of the standard textbooks of psychology no longer ignore the topic or treat it with derision. An increasing number of publications such as the present volume can now address themselves to the serious reader and do not have to cater for the popular or occult market. It is noteworthy that all the authors represented here are able to pursue their interests without let or hindrance either in an academic or medical or educational setting or else in a private research institute on the periphery of a university.

The main barrier to greater acceptance at present is the sheer paucity of first rate data and the relatively minute scale on which research is being conducted so that corroboration by independent workers is the exception rather than the rule. This, in turn, is partly a function of lack of official recognition which prevents parapsychology from receiving its quota in money and manpower which so many other sciences can take for granted. Meanwhile a new danger threatens parapysychology which, ironically, comes, not from the hostility of official science, but from the uncritical enthusiasm of the masses. The retreat from reason is rapidly turning into a stampede; the 'occult revival', to use the current cliché, threatens to engulf even our seats of learning. There is now no topic, it seems, so silly or so intellectually disreputable that it cannot attract large and enthusiastic audiences on the modern campus provided it is purveyed by someone who can command the right sort of charisma. In these circumstances the commercial exploitation and debasement of parapsychological ideas is no less inevitable than the spread of pornography in a sexually permissive society. Already this trend is gaining ground and, if continued unchecked, it could undo the precarious attempts to raise the status and prestige of parapsychology. Parapsychology has, all through its history, suffered from its fatal attraction for persons of unbalanced mind who seek in it their personal salvation; with any relaxation in standards of rigour and objectivity the mischief which such people can do is bound to become aggravated. The paradox of the current situation is that while many of the tangible gains which parapsychology has won in recent years, such as we have already mentioned, are due in part to the greater intellectual permissiveness that now pervades society, if this permissiveness should go too far the result would be disastrous for parapsychology.

Yet, necessary as it is to say these things at the present time, it is also as well to remember that parapsychology cannot lightly disown its hybrid origins. The fact is that while all the sciences have roots that go back into magic and occult beliefs and practices, these are much closer to the surface in the case of parapsychology. Much of the financial support for parapsychology still comes from Spiritualist sources and the religious motivation of many of its adherents and practitioners are thinly disguised. Academic parapsychologists may prefer to work with docile guessing subjects in the hygienic atmosphere of the laboratory but the rare and freakish individuals who are capable of more spectacular feats will always retain their fascination however awkward or troublesome. Any too strenuous attempts to render parapsychology straightforward and innocuous in the interests of respectability are liable to result in stifling its creative elements. Parapsychologists should not be afraid of a certain amount of intellectual slumming and should be ready to consider ideas from whatever source no matter how repugnant to commonsense. This can be done without compromising one's standards of evidence though it does demand an unusual frame of mind, one that can combine a severe critical approach with a lack of fastidiousness in the face of facts. Those who are committed to a belief in the rationality of nature or in the coherence of knowledge are better advised to stick to more orthodox disciplines; parapsychology is for those who have no other allegiance than to the truth.

# 1   Instrumentation in the Parapsychology Laboratory

HELMUT SCHMIDT

## SYNOPSIS

*Automated techniques of measuring and recording and computerised processing of data have already had far reaching effects on nearly all the sciences in recent years. Parapsychologists, however, have, on the whole, been slow to avail themselves of these new technological facilities, preferring to stick to their time honoured routines of card shuffling and dice rolling. The author, who came into parapsychology from a background in physics, is a shining exception. Thanks in no small part to his own work, which has already won wide acclaim, this situation is rapidly changing and the parapsychology laboratory is fast assuming a new look.*

*The idea of using a machine to test ESP is not itself new for, as the author reminds us, G. N. Tyrrell, with his electrical apparatus, set a precedent before World War 2, but the Schmidt machines that are described here, by virtue of their convenience, compactness, portability and so on, and because they are to all intents and purposes foolproof in operation, have advanced the whole art of instrumentation in this field to a new level. For example, they make it possible for the data to be recorded direct onto punch tape thus cutting out all those hazardous intermediate steps involving human intervention.*

*The author starts by discussing some of the special problems that arise in any attempt to obtain a purely objective measurement of a psi effect when, ex hypothesi, the nature of the phenomenon is paranormal or unknown so that even if genuine we cannot always be sure that the subject alone is responsible. He concludes that: 'the main merit of automation in psi research is not the technical convenience and elegance but the possibility to keep human influence other than the subject's out of the picture as far as possible', a point that may become clearer when we discuss the animal research described in Chapter 4.*

*He then goes on to consider some of the systems of randomisation that have been used in the design of guessing machines and points out that the very rapid electronic ring counters that are now available can be relied on to generate almost ideal random sequences. He, himself, however, prefers to exploit nature's own random process as exemplified in certain quantum events. Thus, his original machine, with which he achieved such impressive results, was designed to be triggered off by electrons emitted by the atoms of Strontium 90 in radioactive decay.*

*Next, he turns his attention to the testing of PK and discusses various devices that have been used in this connection from the automatic motor driven die tumbler of J. B. Rhine (1943) to the electronic gadgets which he himself has designed which use subatomic particles as targets. Of special interest here is his own 'random walk' display panel governed by a binary random number generator (RNG) where the subject's task is to try and influence the direction taken by a moving light. A successful experiment using this setup is here illustrated and described. Not the least puzzling aspect of such a setup is that the subject knows nothing about the mechanics of the system he is attempting to influence but concentrates exclusively on the display panel.*

*The question of feedback in PK experiments is then discussed with particular reference to the author's own investigations using a RNG which makes it possible to speed up the frequency of trials far beyond the rate at which the subject can consciously attend to each trial. By converting the hits into audible clicks, the subject can attend instead to the variations in the quickfire sequence of clicks from which he can tell whether his rate of scoring is increasing or decreasing at any given instant. Alternatively, visual feedback can be supplied by letting the hits govern the movements of a recording pen. These techniques have already proved extraordinarily effective in producing highly significant overall scores in a very brief span of time.*

*In his final section the author raises certain theoretical issues concerning the nature of psi and its relationship to known physical laws. He asks, in particular, whether psi operates by modifying only certain statistical laws in physics or whether it also upsets the conservation laws for energy and momentum. The former may be called a 'weak violation' of physical law, the latter a 'strong violation'. He suggests how, if PK involves a weak violation, it might be applied in the case of the Einstein-Podolsky-Rosen paradox. Readers not well versed in the mysteries of quantum theory, however, should not feel too disap-*

*pointed if they find this hard going. Perhaps not the least important point to note about the contents of this chapter is that the evidence for psi continues to mount even when the fullest automation is operating and hence where conditions are at their most stringent.*

*Editor*

## INTRODUCTION

Parapsychology studies a new type of interaction between the human mind and the outside world, an interaction which cannot be accounted for by the present framework of physics. This interaction in the form of telepathy, clairvoyance, precognition or psychokinesis has been observed in the laboratory regularly as a relatively weak effect. But there are some indications that these psychic phenomena can occur in rather strong form in real life situations and occasionally in the laboratory. These indications of strong psychic effects, observed in connection with a few outstanding human subjects, like mediums and public performers, provided the first stimulus for a scientific study. But soon it was found that psychic phenomena in less spectacular form can be displayed by very many subjects. Fortunately these weak psi effects could be demonstrated with very simple tools, dice and playing cards, which nevertheless formed a very sensitive and accurate detecting device for psi (Rhine 1953). The easy availability of these tools was particularly important at the early phases of psi research since most of the work was done by small groups or single individuals who could not spend much effort on elaborate test equipment. Serious attempts to utilise modern instrumentation which has been so extremely helpful in other fields of science like physics or biology were made only fairly recently.

The presently most active efforts in psi research go in two directions. A physics–biology oriented approach tries to understand psi from first principles and tries to isolate the basic natural laws underlying psi effects. Questions to be studied here are how psi fits into the conventional space–time causality pattern, whether psi violates the energy conservation law of physics or is merely a statistical effect, and the question whether psi effects are restricted to animate nature. A psychology oriented approach, on the other hand, studies how psi is related to the personality, whether it has similarities to other cognitive functions, and whether psi performance can be developed.

Both these approaches cover much common ground. Thus the

first two topics to be discussed, the methods for data recording and the psi test machines might have interesting aspects from both viewpoints. The later discussion of the feedback methods might perhaps seem more interesting to the psychologist and the last section might be of primary interest for the physicist.

## DATA RECORDING

In the framework of classical physics the human experimenter played the role of a passive observer, who could just watch without having to disturb nature in the process. With the development of quantum theory, however, it became apparent that an experimenter who wants to obtain information on, say, the structure of an atom, has to disturb the atom rather violently. Furthermore, this inter-action between experimenter and object in the process of observation is not just a practically bothersome feature, but is intrinsically embedded in the theory.

In parapsychology the present situation is different insofar as we do not have a theory. But, as in quantum theory, the process of a measurement seems to be much more than a matter of purely technical relevance.

Let me begin, however, with the more technical aspects of data recording. The need for some objective documentation of test results was already felt at the very early stages of psychic research, when spiritistic seances and other psychic demonstrations produced results which made the onlooker seriously doubt the reliability of his senses. In the earlier statistical laboratory tests the manual recording of the results by one experimenter, or better the independent recording by two experimenters could be considered as reasonably safe but even there the paradoxical nature of psi made some means of fully automatic recording desirable.

For the early researchers the most easily available automatic recording device was photographic equipment. For statistical tests with a very large number of trials this has certainly the disadvantage that the evaluation of the pictures has to be made manually, but still this method has been used occasionally, for example in the psychokinesis experiments reported by R. A. McConnell (McConnell 1955a). In these tests a die tumbler was used, consisting of a motor driven cage which stopped automatically at regular intervals. The cage contained several dice and the subject tried to enforce mentally the appearance of many sixes (or other pre-specified target numbers) whenever the cage stopped. The results of the successive trials were recorded manually, but in addition an automatic camera photographed each outcome. The photographic recording played a more fundamental role in a later experiment (McConnell 1955b). The question to be studied there was whether the psychokinetic effect could act over long distances. For this purpose the PK subject had to be spatially separated from the die tumbler. In addition it also seemed desirable to separate the experimenter from the die tumbler. Otherwise PK results might have been due to a short range PK effect exerted subconsciously by the experimenter. Here, as in many other cases, the automatic recorder is preferable because then we do not have to worry about a possible distortion of the results by a possible PK effect due to the human recorder.

In connection with the development of electric test machines more convenient means of recording became available: for example, data can be printed on punch tape which in turn can be evaluated directly by a computer. Punch tape recording might be most useful for laboratory use where the bulkiness of most punch tape recorders does not matter and the noise produced can be easily shielded. Less noisy and easier to transport is a small ink pen chart recorder. There, however, the data cannot directly be transfered to a computer. On the other hand a recording of the scores on paper charts is particularly useful in cases where the experimenter wants to record also physiological data, like heart rate or brain wave activity on the same chart.

For the experimenter with a working knowledge in electronics the least expensive and in many respects most advantageous means of recording is provided by ordinary magnetic tape recorders. Tape recorders are noiseless, easily transportable and the data can be automatically transferred to a computer. The only disadvantage is that the data cannot be visually checked directly as with the paper-tape or the pen chart recording. Recording on magnetic tape was used for example in a recent PK experiment (Schmidt 1972a) where an electronic random generator (an 'electronic coinflipper') produced a binary sequence of +1s (heads) and −1s (tails) and the subject tried mentally to enforce an increased generation rate of +1s. The +1s and −1s were simply registered as clicks in one or the other channel of a portable stereo tape recorder. The tape could be played back to activate counters for rechecking the total results or to feed a computer for a more detailed analysis. A particular advantage of the magnetic recording in this case was the possibility of high speed operation. A clean recording was possible even when the binary random numbers were generated at the rate of 1000 per second. With slightly more effort the experimenter can record on magnetic tape also much more complex information than just a binary sequence.

The fundamental problems arising in connection with the registration of test results in parapsychology are much less understood than the corresponding problems connected to the measuring process in physics. Thus, instead of giving a logically consistent report I can only illustrate the typical difficulties with the help of examples. Allow me to mention first two rather extreme cases.

1. The recording of data on to photographic film might seem an absolutely reliable method, and actually the photographic records in McConnell's experiments did agree with the manually recorded data whenever such manual recording was done. On the other hand we have reports by Jule Eisenbud (Eisenbud 1967) on his test subject Ted Serios, who could mentally produce pictures on polaroid film, of objects which were not physically present. Taking this possibility of a psychokinesis effect acting on the film seriously, the film loses its absolute reliability as objective recorder.

2. Hans Bender (Bender 1968) reports in connection with the case of the 'Rosenheim Poltergeist', how he attempted, with the help of the physicist Dr. Karger, to study objectively some alleged voltage fluctuations in the power line. Explosions of many lightbulbs in the building had suggested looking for high voltage fluctuations as the common cause. An automatically recording voltmeter connected to the power line did actually show irregular deflections of its indicator needle. To the dismay of the experimenters, however, these deflections still occurred after the instrument was disconnected from the power line, such that voltage fluctuation in the power line could no longer be considered as cause of the needle deflection. Thus we might have here an example of where, in the presence of exceptionally strong PK effects, the readings of the measuring instrument, the voltmeter, lose their meaning as to the quantity to be measured.

These two examples may be considered as somewhat pathological, perhaps, because such drastic PK effects are, to say the least, rather rare. Thus the experimenter in routine psi tests might generally not have to worry that perhaps some direct PK force could move the display needle of some recorder or punch holes into paper tape in improper places. But also quite ordinary psi laboratory experiments indicate that the process of recording and evaluating the data is an integral part of the experiment and may have a significant bearing on the results.

An example is given by the well known experiment by West and Fisk (West, 1953), where the subjects tried to predict numbers (the numbers 1–12 on a clock dial) which were randomly determined by random number tables. This was a mail experiment: the experimenter Fisk mailed sheets to the subjects, the subjects entered their predictions and mailed the sheets back to Fisk. Then Fisk and West divided the alphabetically ordered pile of record sheets, and Fisk checked the first half by matching the guesses against a previously specified part of the random number table, and West checked the other half. The result showed that the subjects whose scores were checked by Fisk scored significantly higher than the subjects whose scores were checked by West. Thus the person who checked the results seemed somehow to have a bearing on the results although the subjects at the time of the test did not know that their results would be split among two different checkers.

Parapsychologists could try to describe the situation in terms of their standard terminology by saying, for example, that the subjects precognitively perceived who would check their sheets and then (as a result of some subconscious psychological bias against one of the experimenters), would score low if they foresaw him as their checker. Without commitment to any such specific explanation it is safe to conclude that the way in which the results were checked after the completion of the precognition test had a bearing on the results.

The main merit of automation in psi research is thus perhaps not the technical convenience and elegance but rather the possibility to keep human influence other than the subject's out of the picture as far as possible. This reduction of the human factor is particularly important with the recent animal experiments which are reported in Randall's article. Automation can certainly not exclude all human influences since we need the human experimenter at least to look at the end results of the experiment.

## RANDOM NUMBER GENERATORS AND PSI TEST MACHINES

The psychic phenomena most regularly observed in the laboratory appear as correlations between the test subject's state of mind (his feelings, guesses, wishes) and external random events. The subject may for example guess some randomly selected ESP card (clairvoyance or telepathy) which is outside the reach of his senses or he may predict the outcome of a future die throw (precognition). In this interaction between subject and outside world the subject does not always appear as a passive receiver of external events (i.e. by ESP) but he can play a more active role and mentally influence the outcome of random events, like the fall of dice (i.e. by PK).

Since most of the observed effects are rather weak such that a careful statistical analysis is required in order to detect the presence of psi, we must be sure that the aforementioned external events are sufficiently random. Let us consider as example a typical clairvoyance test with ESP cards:

The experimenter shuffles a deck of twenty-five ESP cards in the absence of the subject and inserts the pack into an opaque envelope. Next the subject tries to guess the sequence of the cards in the closed envelope and records his guesses. Later the guessed and the actual sequence are compared. Since there are five cards of each of five different types in the ESP deck one would expect that in many such experiments the subjects guess, by pure chance, close to 20% of the cards correctly. The tests show however that some subjects can consistently score slightly more than the expected 20%. In order to interpret these results as due to ESP it is important that the subject has no sensory link to the cards, that the series is long enough to become statistically significant, and that the sequence of the cards after the shuffling can be assumed to be sufficiently random. Although this procedure can, under proper precautions, be considered as fully adequate for establishing the existence of ESP there are good reasons why one might want to automate the procedure with the help of some machine.

## ESP Test Machines

A well known model of such a machine was built by Tyrrell (Tyrrell 1938) in 1938. Instead of the 5 different card symbols the subject had 5 different boxes to choose from. These boxes contained lightbulbs which were connected to a target generator in such a way that only if the subjects opened the 'correct' box the lamp in the box was lit to indicate success. The sequence of the correct boxes was determined by an internal generator for quasi random targets. The machine could be used for telepathy, clairvoyance and precognition tests. In the last case the target was selected after the guess was made, by the random setting of some rotary switch. In connection with this machine Tyrrell used a simple automatic registration device formed by two electrically operated pens which recorded the hits and misses on a paper strip.

With the development of modern electronics easier and more reliable methods for generating random targets became available. In order to build a machine which, for example, can select randomly one out of five choices, we can start with a fast running modulo-5 counter which advances at a very high and regular counting rate (e.g. one million counts per second can be easily handled electronically) in the sequence 1, 2, 3, 4, 5, 1, 2 . . . A random number (1 . . . 5) can then be obtained by stopping the counter suddenly, in whatever position it happens to be, at a *random time*. Due to the high counting frequency the generated number depends very critically on the stopping time, and good randomness can be obtained if the stopping of the counter is triggered manually by the operation of a pushbutton, like in the 'Psi Recorder 70' (Fischer and Hubner 1970). In other machines the random time element is provided by the closure of mechanical relays, like in Tart's ESP tester (Tart 1966) or by similar means (Beloff and Regan 1969).

Nature's most elementary source of randomness is provided by quantum processes which are, according to current physics, in principle random and unpredictable. Let us consider as example the radioactive decay of the nucleus in a Strontium-90 atom. This nucleus is unstable, it can decay at any time, but the average lifetime of a nucleus is approximately 90 years, similar to the average lifetime of people. Unlike people, however, the nucleus does not change with age. No matter how close we look at the nuclei, they all look alike and there seems to be no causal mechanism which determines when the particular atom will decay. That depends rather on pure chance. It was certainly one of the boldest steps of modern physics to take the possibility of pure chance (as opposed to the strict causality of classical physics) as a basic element in nature seriously.

In view of this current interpretation that the decay occurs purely randomly without traceable cause it seems particularly interesting to see if human subjects can predict these decays better than quantum theory permits. The particular interest of quantum processes for parapsychology was first emphasised by Beloff and Evans (1961) in connection with psychokinesis experiments which I will discuss later. The most extensive use of quantum processes in precognition tests was made in my own experiments (Schmidt 1969, Schmidt and Pantas 1972).

In these experiments a Geiger tube mounted next to a small sample of Strontium-90, registered the irregular arrivals of electrons from the radioactive decays. The random arrival times of the electrons served to stop a high frequency modulo-4 counter thus generating randomly the numbers 1, 2, 3, or 4 (see Figure 1.1).

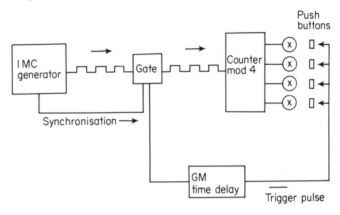

Figure 1.1    Block diagram for the four choice precognition tester.
Signals from a pulse generator pass through a gate and advance a modulo-4 counter at the rate of one million steps per second, in the sequence 1, 2, 3, 4, 1, 2...
If the gate is closed at a random time, then the counter stops randomly in one of its four possible positions. Thus a random number, 1, 2, 3 or 4, is generated and displayed by the lighting of one of four lamps.
The random time is provided with the help of a Geiger-Müller tube which registers the arrivals of electrons emitted randomly from a radioactive sample of Strontium 90, at an average rate of approximately ten per second.
When a button is pushed the G.M. tube is activated such that the arrival of the next following electron triggers the closing of the gate. A blocking device (synchronisation) ensures that the gate is not closed while the counter is in the process of advancing since this might lead to improper electronic operation.

During the test the subject sat in front of a small panel with four coloured lamps, four corresponding pushbuttons and two electro-mechanical reset counters (see Figure 1.2). Before a button was pressed the lamps were dark and the internal counter advanced rapidly in the sequence 1, 2, 3, 4, 1 ... When a button was pressed nothing happened until the next electron reached the Geiger tube. At this moment the internal counter was stopped and the stopping position was displayed to the subject by the lighting of one of the four lamps. The test subjects guessed repeatedly which lamp would light next and registered the guess by pressing the corresponding button. If the lamp lit shortly afterwards was the one next

Figure 1.2 Experimenter and subject with the precognition test machine.

to the pressed button a hit was recorded by one of the reset counters and the other counter recorded the number of trials made. In addition, the complete sequences of guesses and targets were automatically recorded on paper punch tape. With this arrangement many test series giving evidence for the existence of precognition were made. But still, even with such a psychologically and technically advantageous test machine the experimenter had to make considerable efforts in preselecting the subjects and exploring the best working conditions for each subject, before consistent results were obtained (*see* Figure 1.3).

## PK Test Machines

A new challenge to machine builders was provided by the statistical psychokinesis tests begun by J.B. Rhine (Rhine 1953) where the subjects tried mentally to influence the fall of dice thrown from a cup. After these tests had indicated that some subjects are able to obtain a desired die face with above chance frequency, the test conditions were improved by the use of the already mentioned automatic die tumbler with the motor driven cage (Rhine 1943). The observed effect persisted under these tightened conditions, and since then a large number of tests has been done with this machine, tests with one and with many dice, tests with one and with several subjects, and also the test mentioned previously by McConnell where the die positions were photographically recorded. A new design for PK tests with dice was introduced by Cox in the 'placement tests' (Cox 1951). The dice were made to roll down an

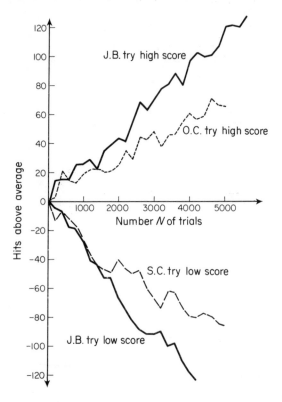

Figure 1.3    Results of a precognition test with the three subjects who had per-
formed particularly well in previous tests.
In this test the subjects had the option to aim either for a large or for a small number of coincidences between the button pushed and the lamp lit. In the latter case they tried to push a button next to any lamp which would not light.
Among a total number of 20 000 trials made, 10 672 trials aiming for a high score gave 7·1% more coincidences than expected by chance. The other trials, aiming for a low score, gave 9·1% fewer coincidences than chance expectancy. Thus under both conditions the subjects obtained what they were aiming for, an increased or decreased number of 'hits'.
The figure gives the cumulative number of hits, above chance (plotted after each block of 200 trials) for each subject. The subject J.B. (a 'spiritistic medium') worked under both conditions, while O.C. (a truckdriver and amateur psychic) and S.C. (his 16 year old daughter) operated only under one condition each, corresponding to their personal preference.

incline onto a tabletop, and the subjects tried mentally to deflect the rolling dice to the right or to the left. Particularly consistent results were reported with the Swedish engineer Forwald as subject (Forwald 1954, Rhine 1970). Forwald also made an interesting attempt to measure the 'psychic force' acting on the dice in quantitative physical units (dynes). After he had obtained in extended tests a certain, statistically significant, average deflection of the dice in the desired direction he estimated how much mechanical force would be required to produce the same average deflection. Forwald's interesting discussion, however, does not necessarily imply that PK can be considered as a force comparable to electrical or gravitational forces.

A large number of mechanical and electromechanical test machines were constructed in the hope of finding some machine which would be particularly suitable for the demonstration of PK, and to find possible limits for the range of PK. Thus E. Cox (Rhine 1970) built machines for tests in which subjects tried to change the conductivity of salt solution, to deflect the waterdrops emerging from a shower nozzle, or to influence the closing rate of electromechanical relays. Furthermore, Cox experimented with large numbers of dice or steel balls which the subjects tried to influence simultaneously.

For the study of distance as a possible physical limit to PK, McConnell used the automatic arrangement mentioned before, where experimenter and subject were spatially separated from the target dice. Aimed also towards the study of possible limits for PK was an experiment by Beloff and Evans in which the subjects tried mentally to affect the decay rate of radioactive nuclei (Beloff and Evans 1961). The authors note that the radioactive decay of nuclei is not only a purely random process as mentioned before, but that even for the physicist it is extremely difficult to influence in any way the decay rate. Thus, for example, all electric or magnetic fields which physicists are able to produce leave the nucleus practically undisturbed.

In the experimental setup a source of alpha particles was mounted inside a counter (to catch all particles irrespective of their direction) and the arriving particles were individually counted and their number displayed to the subject. In the PK test the subject tried first for one minute to increase the counting frequency, and then for another minute to decrease it. Tests with thirty students did not give evidence for a PK effect, but, whereas the subjects' task was rather straightforward and easy to explain, the feedback display in form of the numbers of received particles might not have been sufficiently stimulating for optimal results.

In my own later experiments (Schmidt 1971) I used a possibly more stimulating display, although the basic task was less easy to explain and to visualise. The results showed, however, that human subjects *are* able to influence mentally a random device based on radioactive decays. In my arrangement a sequence of binary numbers, of +1s and −1s is generated by a process similar to the one used in the described precognition tester. An electronic switch oscillates at a very high rate (a million times per second) between a +1 and a −1 position. The oscillation is stopped when the next radioactive decay particle is received by a Geiger tube and the stopping position determines the random number, +1 or −1. The subject's task, which is to make the next particle arrive at the Geiger counter (with the accuracy of $10^{-6}$ seconds) just at the time when the switch is in, say, the +1 position, may sound discouragingly complicated, but generally the subjects are not aware of these details. The subjects rather concentrate on the display given by a panel with a circular arrangement of 9 lamps (*see* Figure 1.4). One of the lamps is lit at a time and whenever a

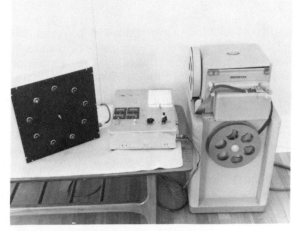

Figure 1.4    Binary random generator (centre) with lamp display panel (left) and punch tape recorder (right).

+1 or −1 is produced the light jumps by step in clockwise or counterclockwise direction respectively. Thus the subject tries mentally to enforce an overall clockwise motion on the random walk of the light. The jumps occur at a rate of, typically, one per second such that the subject can concentrate on each individual event. Evidence for PK was observed with this arrangement in several tests with slightly preselected subjects (*see* Figure 1.5). A further successfully operating PK device will be mentioned in the next section.

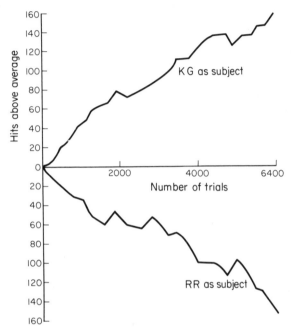

Figure 1.5   Result of a P.K. test with two preselected subjects.
These subjects, an outgoing girl (K.G.) and a quiet South-American ESP researcher (R.R.) had produced rather consistent scores in previous tests: K.G. had been successful in moving the light in the circular display in the desired direction, whereas with R.R. the light had shown a significant tendency to move opposite to the subject's concious wish. Such a PK missing tendency, if it is persistent enough, can serve as well as PK hitting for demonstrating the existence of PK.

The results of this experiment confirmed the scoring tendencies of the two subjects, each of which contributed a total of 6400 trials (50 runs of 128 trials). The figure shows the increase of the cumulative score (plotted after each block of 256 trials) with the number of trials. Both subjects scored rather regularly in the expected direction. The odds against obtaining by chance such a large difference between the scores of the two subjects is more than 10 million to one.

## FEEDBACK METHODS

The question whether psi performance can be trained with a proper feedback has often been raised, but so far no reliable teaching system seems to be available, and furthermore Tart (Tart 1966) pointed out that the standard test methods are psychologically not favourable for psi development. And, even though some of the electronic test machines already mentioned combined with a large variety of possible feedback devices may seem more suitable for psi teaching, these machines might still have two disadvantages. First, the immediate feedback might interrupt the subject's concentration and upset his mental state. Second, the low reliability of the feedback may be misleading to the subject. This is certainly true in cases where the subject scores only slightly above chance. Since in that case most of the hits will be due to chance, a hit does not give strong evidence that the subject's psi was operating.

A natural way out of these difficulties might be provided by tests with higher trial frequency. Particularly suited for high speed operation are PK tests because there the subject does not have to make any motor response which would limit the speed. Consider as example the already mentioned PK test where a sequence of binary numbers, +1s and −1s, was generated at speeds of 30 per second and 300 per second respectively (Schmidt 1972).

At these high speeds the subject has not much time to concentrate on the individual events, but still psychologically meaningful displays are possible. So far significant PK effects were obtained with an acoustical and with an optical type of feedback. In the first case the subject wore headphones and the +1s and −1s were displayed as clicks in the right or left ear respectively. The subject's task was to try mentally to enforce an increased clicking rate in the specified target ear. At the operation speed of 30 per second the subjects could still distinguish the individual clicks, whereas at the rate of 300 per second the subjects noted only statistical volume fluctuations between the two ears and could just concentrate on obtaining an increased sound volume in the target ear. In the tests with visual display the subject looked at the pen of an ink chart recorder. At the start of the test the pen was at the centreline of the paper chart. During the test run the deflection of the pen to the right or left was proportional to the accumulated difference between the generated +1s and −1s. The subject's task was to try mentally to make the pen move during a short run as far as possible in a specified direction. One might hope that under these conditions a subject could learn to cultivate some mental state which is conducive for high scoring. So far it has only been shown that PK can be rather efficiently displayed in this manner, but no systematic approach towards the learning problem has been made yet.

The last mentioned display is quite similar to some displays used for biofeedback training: there, as in the attempts at psi training, the subject has to learn some skill which is originally not susceptible to his conscious control. Elmer Green's subjects (Green 1970), for example, wanted to learn to increase the surface temperature of the skin, for the purpose of enhancing relaxation. This learning is facilitated by feedback through an instrument needle which displays the present skin temperature. The subject who does not know primarily how to approach the task is asked just to concentrate on moving the display needle to the right, corresponding to an increase in skin temperature. This and other biofeedback methods for the control of primarily unconscious body functions work surprisingly well, but whether the corresponding psi feedback methods are effective for psi learning remains to be seen.

The use of biofeedback methods in connection with psi tests will be discussed in more detail by Honorton (*see* Chapter 2). Most of the mentioned psi feedback methods are not directly applicable for tests with animals, but the standard method of reward and punishment used in animal psychology can be adapted. This will be discussed by Randall (*see* Chapter 3).

## MEASUREMENT OF THE PHYSICAL ASPECTS OF PSI

The psychic interaction between the human mind and the outside world shows some characteristic features which set it apart from the types of interactions familiar to the physicist. Thus for example the results of clairvoyance or telepathy experiments seem to be rather independent of the distance between the receiver and the object or the sender. Furthermore, the existence of precognition indicates that this interaction couples the present state of mind of the subject with some event which has not yet occurred. I might mention here that some types of such 'noncausal' interactions, in spite of their intuitively implausible appearance have been studied occasionally by theoretical physicists who are used to dealing with concepts outside the range of our everyday intuition.

Before going much further into this very involved problem of causality one might want to see somewhat clearer to what extent psi is inconsistent with the framework of conventional physics. Since most of the reported psi effects are of a statistical nature one might ask in particular whether psi does affect only the statistical laws of physics whereas other laws like the conservation laws for energy and momentum remain intact.

This fundamental question might be approached from two directions:

1. One could start from the working hypothesis that PK does violate the familiar conservation laws for energy or momentum and one could try to confirm this by a properly designed PK test. With the methods of modern physics even quite minute effects could be observed. For high precision tests one would best work at very low temperatures such that the thermal energy fluctuations become smaller than the possibly observable energy changes due to PK. I will not, however, go into the details of the many tests which one might consider particularly interesting.

2. The other approach starts from the working hypothesis that psi effects 'only' the statistical laws of physics. I want to show that this approach which might seem to provide the smoothest incorporation of psi into the established framework of physics, can have, nevertheless, some rather drastic, experimentally testable implications. These are related to the famous Einstein-Podolsky-Rosen paradox (Einstein 1935) which played a major role in the discussions concerning the proper interpretation of quantum theory. Let me explain this with the help of a somewhat idealised specific example.

Positronium is an atom-like system formed by an electron and a positron orbiting around each other. This system is not stable. Shortly after its formation, the electron and positron annihilate each other, with emission of two photons in opposite directions. Each of these photons, taken by itself, is unpolarised. If, therefore, one of the photons encounters say, a vertically oriented polarising filter set up by an experimenter, A, the photon will make a 'quantum jump' into the vertically or horizontally polarised state and correspondingly the experimenter will find the quantum transmitted through or reflected by the filter. Each of these two possibilities occurs with the same probability 1/2.

Let us assume next that there is another experimenter B on the other side of the positronium who measures the polarisation of the other photon of the pair. Then, in agreement with quantum theory and with experimental observation, this second photon is always found to be polarised orthogonally to the first one. Thus, if A and B set up horizontally polarised filters then precisely one of the photons will pass the filter and the other will not. The EPR paradox arises because, according to quantum theory, the photon does not make the decision whether to pass the filter at, say, A, until it arrives at A. This leaves the embarrassing question: 'how can the photon at B know instantly of the decision made by the photon at A such as to behave correspondingly?' A thorough discussion shows that the situation, while intuitively implausible, is not logically inconsistent, and, in particular, it can be shown that within the framework of conventional physics this setup cannot serve as a means of instantaneous information transmission from A to B.

The situation changes, however, if there is a PK subject at A who can influence the quantum jumps of the arriving photons such that an increased number of photons passes the filter. Assuming that PK does not violate the conservation law for the aforementioned coupling between the two photons, the number of photons passing through the filter at B should become correspondingly reduced, and an observer at B should notice instantaneously when the subject at A turns on his PK effort. Thus we would have a means of instantaneous information transmission.

This example could be easily cast into an experimentally more manageable form. (The photons in this case have very high energies and are therefore difficult to polarise.) The example should show that even a 'weak violation' of the statistical laws only, might have interesting implications which would even suggest some means of channelling the PK effect out of the laboratory at A to some distant location B.

Thus the question to what extent psi violates the laws of conventional physics, in either a 'weak' or a 'strong' sense, together with the question of the causal structure of psi, might form an interesting field of future research for the physicist with his sophisticated equipment in combination with the parapsychologist with his experience in creating psychologically favourable conditions for the observation of psi.

## APPENDIX: Electronic Details of Random Number Generator

The RNG was built from three types of microcircuits: inverters, gates, and flipflops (Fairchild F$\mu$L 90029, F$\mu$L 91529, F$\mu$L 92629). Two logical voltage levels are given by a positive voltage ($\sim$2 V), the logical '1', and a near zero (ground) voltage, the logical '0'.

The logical functions of inverters and gates are indicated in Figure 1.6. The inverter has a positive output only if the input is near zero potential. The gate has a positive output only if all three inputs are near zero potential.

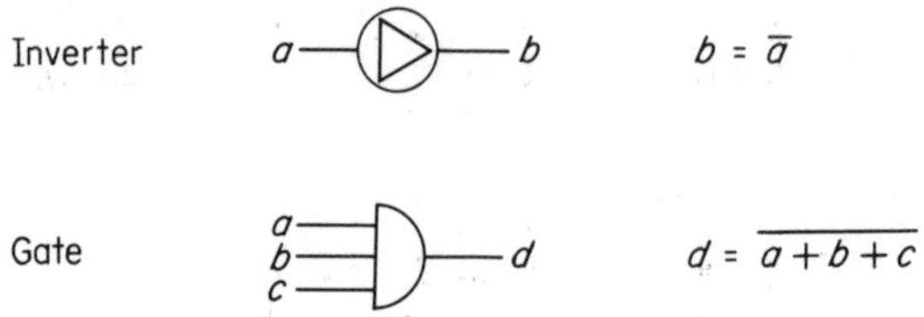

Inverter    $a$—▷—$b$        $b = \bar{a}$

Gate    $\begin{matrix} a \\ b \\ c \end{matrix}$⎤⎞—$d$        $d = \overline{a + b + c}$

Figure 1.6    Logic functions of inverter and gate, expressed in the notation of Boolean algebra. Inputs at left.

The flipflop (Figure 1.7) has two possible states. In one state the output $O_1$ is positive and the output $O_2$ grounded. The five inputs T,

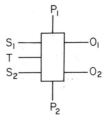

Figure 1.7    Flipflop with five inputs and the outputs $O_1$ and $O_2$.

$S_1$, $S_2$, $P_1$, $P_2$ have the following function. A 'downgoing' pulse (input voltage which changes sufficiently rapidly from a positive level to near ground level) applied at T flips the flipflop, interchanging the voltages at $O_1$ and $O_2$. An 'upgoing' pulse fed into T does not change the state of the flipflop.

A rapidly downgoing pulse (an upgoing pulse has no effect) fed simultaneously into T and $S_1$ has the same effect as any positive (slow or fast rising) pulse fed into $P_1$ in that both leave the flipflop with positive voltage at $O_1$. (If $O_1$ is already positive, nothing is changed; if $O_2$ was positive the system is flipped.) The connections $S_2$, $P_2$, and $O_2$ function symmetrically to $S_1$, $P_1$, and $O_1$.

The complete circuit diagram of the RNG is given by Figures 1.8a and b. Consider first Figure 1.8a and assume that a short positive pulse has been applied to the 'reset' line (at left in

Figure 1.8a) and that the 'set' line is at positive potential. Then the output $\alpha$ of the flipflop $F_1$ is positive and the gates $G_1 \ldots G_4$ are

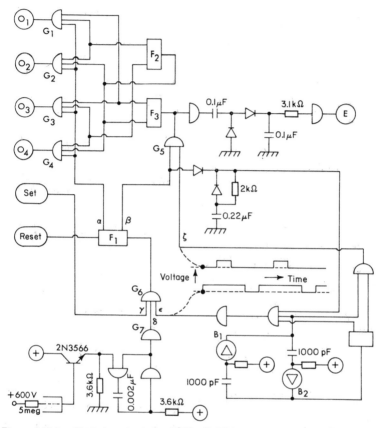

Figure 1.8(a)   Central part of the RNG. $\oplus$ This point is connected to $+3V$; $\textcircled{E}$ This point is connected to the point with the same symbol somewhere else in the diagrams of Figure 1.8a and 1.8b.

closed (the outputs $0_1 \ldots 0_4$ are grounded). These gates, combined with the flipflops $F_2$ and $F_3$ form a modulo-4 counter.

The two inverters $B_1$ and $B_2$, combined with two capacitors and two resistors (the latter are built into the inverter elements), form a 1 MHz squarewave generator. With the help of a flipflop and three gates, two different rectangular waves, as indicated in Figure 1.8a, are fed into the input $\zeta$ and $\epsilon$ of $G_5$ and $G_6$. The wave entering $G_5$ is there inverted and drives the modulo-4 counter.

The wave entering $G_6$ cannot pass this gate, because of the positive potential of the 'set' line.

This situation, where the modulo-4 counter advances very rapidly but no signal reaches the outputs $0_1 \ldots 0_4$ because the output gates $G_1 \ldots G_4$ are closed, persists as long as no button is pressed.

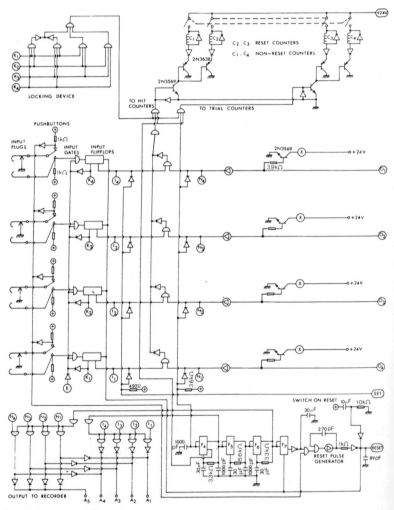

Figure 1.8(b)    RNG circuitry continued. The diagrams of Figure 1.8a and 1.8b (connected via $0_1 \ldots 0_4$, E and the set and reset line) give the complete circuit.

The Geiger-Müller tube registers electrons from a Strontium 90 source at the average rate of 10 particles per second. Each count triggers a one-shot pulse generator to send a positive pulse of $10^{-5}$ s duration into $G_7$. This in turn grounds the input $\delta$ of $G_6$ for $10^{-5}$ s.

If a button is pressed, the 'set' input of $G_6$ is grounded and this gate gives a positive output as soon as simultaneously an incoming electron has grounded (for $10^{-5}$ s) the gate input $\delta$ and furthermore, the input $\epsilon$ of $G_6$ is at ground level. Note that the latter condition is satisfied only at times when the modulo-4 counter is not in the process of switching (the counter switches when the input voltage at $F_3$ goes down, i.e. when the input voltage at $\zeta$ of $G_5$ rises).

The positive output from $G_6$ actuates the flipflop $F_1$, closes gate $G_5$ (providing a clean cut of the wave train entering the modulo-4 counter), stops the modulo-4 counter, and opens the output gates $G_1 \ldots G_4$. At this stage one of the outputs (corresponding to the stopping position of the modulo-4 counter) carries a positive voltage and lights one of the four panel lamps (Figure 1.8b), displaying the generated random number.

If the button, which was pressed in order to generate a random number, is released, the 'set' line again assumes a positive potential and a short positive pulse enters the 'reset' line. This flips $F_1$, closes $G_1 \ldots G_4$, opens $G_5$, and lets the modulo-4 counter proceed counting until the next button is pressed.

Figure 1.8b completes the diagram of the RNG. If one of the push-buttons (left in the Figure) is pressed, the corresponding input flipflop is 'set' and the four input gates are closed, such that no other flipflop can be set simultaneously. (If ever two or more of the input flipflops should be set simultaneously the counters are shut off by a locking device.)

The input flipflops act as clean electronic switches which lock the input until a reset pulse arrives.

When a random number is generated, one of the panel lamps lights, the counter for the number of trials advances, and the counter for the number of hits registers a count provided the lamp lit corresponds to the input flipflop set. Furthermore, a pulse enters the delay line beginning at the flipflop $F_4$. If the button is pressed only momentarily and has already been released, the pulse leaving the delay line triggers the reset pulse generator, resetting the RNG in the starting position. If the button is pressed for a prolonged time, the reset occurs as soon as all buttons are released.

The manually operated pushbuttons can be replaced by external input relays which may be operated electronically. This is desirable for statistical tests of the RNG.

The RNG is equipped with five external outputs $A_1 \ldots A_5$ through which the sequence of the buttons pressed and the numbers generated can be transferred to a recording device. After a random number has been generated, one of the outputs $A_1 \ldots A_4$ emits a short pulse, indicating which button has been pressed. Then, $10^{-1}$ s after the end of this pulse, two additional pulses are emitted simultaneously, from $A_5$ and from one of the outputs $A_1 \ldots A_4$. The former identifies the signal as a random number while the latter indicates which random number was generated. The flipflops $F_4 \ldots F_7$ provide the proper duration ($10^{-1}$ s) and spacing of these pulses.

## REFERENCES

Beloff, J., and Evans, L. (1961) 'A Radioactive Test of Psychokinesis.' *J. Soc. Psych. Res.*, **41**, 41

Beloff, J., and Regan, T. (1969) 'The Edinburgh Electronic ESP Tester.' *J. Soc. Psych. Res.*, **45**, 7–13

Bender, H. (1968) 'Der Rosenheimer Spuk-Ein Fall Spontaner Psychokinese.' *Zeitschr, f. Parapsych.*, **11**, 104–112

Cox, W. E. (1951) 'The Effect of PK on the Placement of Falling Objects.' *J. Parapsych.*, **15**, 40–48

Einstein, A., Podolsky, B., and Rosen, N. (1935) *Phys. Rev.*, **47**, 777

Eisenbud, J. (1967) *The World of Ted Serios*, Morrows, New York

Fischer, D., and Hubner, H. (1970) 'Psirecorder 70.' *Zeitschr. f. Parapsych.*, **12**, 42–59 (in German)

Forwald, H. (1954) 'An Approach to Instrumental Investigation of Psychokinesis.' *J. Parapsych.*, **18**, 219–233

Green, E., Green, A., and Walters, E. (1970) 'Voluntary Control of Internal States: Psychological and Physiological.' *J. Transpersonal Psych.*, **2**, 1–26

McConnell, R. A. (1955a) 'Wishing With Dice.' *J. Exper. Psych.*, **50**, 269–275

McConnell, R. A. (1955b) 'Remote Night Test for PK.' *J. Amer. Soc. Psych. Res.*, **49**, 99–108

Rhine, J. B. (1943) 'Dice Thrown by Cup and by Machine in PK Tests.' *J. Parapsych.*, **7**, 207–217

Rhine, J. B. (1953) *New World of the Mind*, Sloane, New York

Rhine, L. (1970) *Mind over Matter*, Macmillan, New York

Schmidt, H. (1969) 'Quantum Processes Predicted?' *New Scientist*, 16 Oct., 114–115

Schmidt, H. (1971) 'Mental Influence on Random Events.' *New Scientist*, 24 June, 757–758

Schmidt, H. (1973) 'PK Test with a High Speed Random Number Generator.' *J. Parapsych.*, **37,** 105–118

Schmidt, H., and Pantas, L. (1972) 'PK Tests with Internally Different Machines.' *J. Parapsych.*, **36,** 222–232

Tart, C. (1966) 'ESP A Tester: An Automatic Testing Device for Parapsychological Research.' *J. Amer. Soc. Psych. Res.*, **60,** 256–269

Tyrrell, G. N. M. (1938) 'The Tyrrell Apparatus for Testing Extra-Sensory Perception.' *J. Parapsych.*, **2,** 107–118

West, D. J., and Fisk, G. W. (1953) 'A Dual ESP Experiment with Clock Cards.' *J. Soc. Psych. Res.*, **37,** 185–197

# 2 ESP and Altered States of Consciousness

**CHARLES HONORTON***

## SYNOPSIS

*When one considers how large a part hypnosis and trance medium-ship played in the pioneer investigations of the last century, to say nothing of the role of dreams in the study of spontaneous phenomena, one may wonder whether the new found interest in 'altered states of consciousness' among parapsychologists is not rather a reversion to an earlier state of affairs than a 'new direction'. There are, however, two good reasons for regarding such an interest as topical.*

*In the first place, psychology itself has at last begun to cast off its behaviourist inhibitions and to pay attention once again to subjective experiences and introspective reports. The Rhine' school of parapsychology sought to beat behaviourism at its own game by showing that antibehaviourist conclusions could be arrived at on the basis of impeccably objectivist data. But, now that behaviourism is itself on the defensive, parapsychologists feel that they can afford to be broader and more generous in their methods and approach.*

*Secondly, and more importantly, the instrumentation and techniques necessary for measuring and recording physiological changes accompanying changes in mental state have made enormous strides in recent years with the result that many problems connected with states of consciousness can now be tackled without having to rely exclusively on the subject's own testimony. In particular, progress in electroencephalography has opened up all kinds of new possibilities for experimental investigation. For example, the discovery in the late 1950s that rapid eye movements (REMs) afforded a reliable index of dreaming made it possible for the first time to ascertain accurately when the subject was entering upon or emerging from a given dream period. Similarly, physiological changes occurring during trance states, during deep relaxation or during meditation of the yoga or Zen*

* The preparation of this paper was supported in part by United States Public Health Service Research Grant MH-21628–01, National Institute of Mental Health.

*variety can now be objectively assessed and used to corroborate subjective reports. More recently still, the technique known as 'biofeedback' enables the subject to monitor his own internal physiological changes and eventually bring them under control even though normally they are not susceptible to voluntary effort.*

*In this chapter the author, a well known member of the research team of the Maimonides Medical Center, presents, to start with, a chronological survey of the twelve formal experiments so far completed at their Dream Laboratory. By any standards, this work deserves to rank among the most outstanding achievements of parapsychology during the past decade. He then turns to experiments in hypnotism and to the much debated issue of the relevance of hypnosis to psi. Although he cites some tantalising experimental evidence, some of it from his own work, which encourages the view that hypnosis can facilitate ESP performance it is also clear that we do not know as yet why this is so or what the real relationship is.*

*In a final section, the author discusses the connection between brain states characterised by a high incidence of alpha rhythm and ESP scoring, a problem to which he has already made important contributions. He also discusses the use of biofeedback to enable the subject to regulate to some extent the incidence of alpha rhythm. He has found that the subjects who score best in their ESP tests are those whose brain states undergo the greatest shift from an initial state characterised by a low incidence of alpha to an end state characterised by a high incidence. On the basis of such evidence the author concludes by putting forward two hypotheses which, though still very tentative, are likely to have important repercussions on future research :*

*The first, which we may call the 'withdrawal' hypothesis asserts that : 'success in extrasensory tasks will be augmented by attenuation of externally directed attentive activity'. The second, which we may call the 'state-shift' hypothesis asserts that: 'relatively large and rapid shifts in state will be associated with enhanced ESP performance'.*

*Editor*

Are there identifiable mental states particularly conducive to extrasensory perception? Historically, presumptive parapsychological occurrences have been frequently associated with such constructs as 'mediumistic trance,' 'motor automatism,' 'hypnosis,' 'meditation,' and 'dreaming' (Dingwall, 1967; Myers, 1902; Prabhavananda and Isherwood, 1953; L. E. Rhine, 1962). Until recently however, little systematic research has been directed toward the elucidation of subjective states associated with paranormal functioning (White, 1964). In view of the behaviouristic *zeitgeist* it is perhaps not surprising that early proponents of the card-guessing paradigm (Rhine, 1934) largely disregarded their subjects' internal states and focused instead on relatively gross behavioural criteria such as general health, effects of novel stimuli, and the presence of unfamiliar observers.

## PROBLEMS, STRATEGIES AND DEFINITIONS

As early as 1883, Sir Francis Galton wrote caustically of introspection, 'Many persons, especially women and intelligent children, take pleasure in introspection' (Galton, 1883). Inferences concerning mental states have traditionally been dependent upon subjects' verbal reports. While criticisms of introspectionism are numerous and well known, the most serious problem is that it did not lead anywhere (Boring, 1953).

The development of sensitive psychophysiological monitoring equipment and techniques, especially during the last decade, has led to a renewal of scientific interest in states of consciousness and their exploration (Tart, 1968). Using psychophysiological studies of dream recall as an illustration, Stoyva and Kamiya (1968) suggest a new strategy for the investigation of consciousness. They argue that combined use of physiological measures and verbal reports represent *converging operations* which provide a more reliable basis for making inferences about subjective states. Converging operations are '. . . any set of two or more experimental operations which allow the selection or elimination of alternative hypotheses or concepts which could explain an experimental result' (Garner, Hake and Ericksen, 1956). Since they are not perfectly correlated, they can 'converge' upon a single construct.

The term *altered state(s) of consciousness* will be used to denote:

'. . . any mental state, induced by various . . . maneuvers or agents, which can be recognized subjectively . . . (or by an objective observer . . . ) as representing a sufficient deviation in subjective experience or psychological functioning from certain general norms for that individual during alert, waking consciousness. This sufficient deviation may be represented by a greater preoccupation than usual with internal sensations or mental processes, changes in the formal characteristics of thought, and impairment of reality testing to various degrees' (Ludwig, 1966).

It must be emphasised that 'state' constructs are properly invoked as descriptions, not as explanations (Hilgard, 1969). I shall take the position that justification for invoking 'state' constructs increases as the number of converging measures is increased (Miller, 1959).

Thus far, ASC mediated ESP effects have been explored most systematically in dreaming, hypnosis, and what might be termed protomeditative states associated with the presence of electroencephalographic (EEG) alpha rhythm activity. The emphasis of this chapter will therefore be placed on reviewing research in these areas.

## EXTRASENSORY EFFECTS IN DREAMS

### State-specific characteristics of dreaming

Dreaming is a naturally occurring ASC, usually associated with rapid eye movement (REM) sleep, and accounts for approximately 25% of human sleep time. Among the more prominent physiological concomitants of dreaming are low voltage mixed frequency EEG patterns, rapid conjugate eye movements (REMs), diminution of muscle tonus, marked variability of pulse and respiration, and penile erection (Hartmann, 1967). The experiential dimension of dreaming—characterised by Freud as 'the royal road to the unconscious'—is associated with vivid sensory imagery, continuation of daytime thoughts and experiences ('day residue'), predominance of primary process thinking, and symbolisation. One of the most striking findings of recent dream research is the relative difficulty of influencing dream content through sensory stimulation (Tart, 1965).

### Dream-mediated psi—spontaneous cases

Examination of a large sample ($N = 7 119$) of spontaneous ESP experiences* (L. E. Rhine, 1962) implicates dreaming as the most frequently reported vehicle of ESP mediation, accounting for approximately 65% of the cases. Furthermore, 85% of the dream

---

* Interpretation of spontaneous case material is, of course, limited by the degree to which the sample may be regarded as representative. Furthermore, no claim may be made regarding the authenticity of the cases. While this study is consistent with other spontaneous case surveys, it is employed here to illustrate a point about psi processing and is not independently evidential.

experiences but less than half of the waking experiences provided complete—as opposed to fragmented or distorted—information about the external 'target' situation.

This data (Table 2.1) suggests an interaction between states of consciousness (in this case, dreaming versus waking) and quality (signal to noise ratio) of psi experience.

TABLE 2.1   Spontaneous cases related to state of consciousness

| Reported Amount of Information Concerning Target Person/Event | Reported State of Consciousness | | |
|---|---|---|---|
| | Dreaming | Waking | |
| Complete | 3903 | 1241 | 5144 |
| Incomplete | 696 | 1279 | 1975 |
| | 4599 | 2520 | 7119 |

Note: Chi-square ($\chi^2$) = 10·83 (1 df), $P < 0.001$. (Data from Rhine, 1962; Table 1, p. 93).

## Dream-mediated psi—clinical observations

A substantial clinical literature has also developed (Devereaux, 1953), suggesting the occurrence of 'telepathic' dreams within the context of the psychotherapeutic situation. Often striking correspondences have been reported between patients' dreams and contemporaneous events in the private lives of their therapists.

## An experimental approach

In 1960, exploratory pilot studies were initiated by Ullman which led to an experimental analogue to spontaneous dream-mediated psi effects. (For a review of this preliminary work, see Ullman and Krippner, 1970.) A standard methodology emerged which has been applied in a series of formal experiments involving electrophysiological monitoring of subjects throughout the night. During each dream (REM) period, an experimenter actuates a one-way signal to a sensorially isolated agent ('sender') located in a distant room or building (ranging between 60 ft and 45 miles from the sleeping subject (see Figures 2.1 and 2.2). The agent concentrates during this period on a randomly selected target picture and attempts to telepathically influence the content of the subject's dreams. At the end of each dream period, the subject is awakened and gives a tape recorded dream report. In the morning, a post sleep interview is conducted to elicit additional elaboration and associations for each dream.

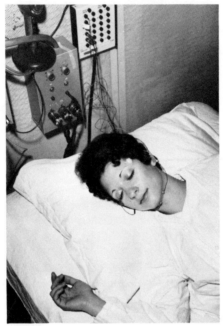

Figure 2.1 A subject sleeping in a soundproof, shielded room, with scalp and eye electrodes permitting investigators in an adjacent room to monitor EEG and eye movement patterns and detect periods of dreaming (Stage REM sleep).

At the end of an experimental series (ranging from 7–32 nights), dream transcripts and copies of the target pictures are sent to a group of judges who 'blindly' (without knowledge of which picture was used as target for a particular night) and independently rate the degree of correspondence between them (usually on a 100-point scale). The mean correct-pair ratings (e.g., target for night 1 and dreams for night 1) are compared statistically with the mean incorrect-pair ratings (e.g., target for night 1 and dreams for nights 2, 3, . . . n) by analysis of variance or binomial ('critical ratio') tests. In most studies, subjects also blind-match target–transcript material. The specific results for each study, along with procedural and other modifications, are summarised below.

**Series I. Screening study.** The initial experiment (Ullman, Krippner and Feldstein, 1966) served as a screening device for selecting subjects for more intensive study. Twelve young adults participated for one night each. Two agents served on alternate nights. Analysis of variance of the judges' ratings did not yield overall statistical significance, although there was a significant ($P < 0.05$) difference favouring one agent. Subject judging, on the other hand, yielded overall significance ($P < 0.05$).

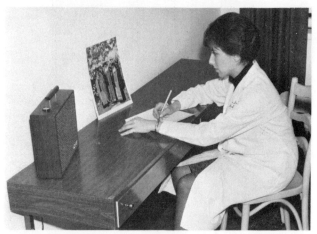

Figure 2.2    An agent (or 'sender'), located in a distant room, concentrates upon a target picture during the subject's dream periods in an attempt to telepathically influence dream content.

**Series II. First selected subject.**    The most promising subject from Series I was paired with the more successful agent in a seven-night study (Ullman, Krippner and Feldstein, 1966). Analysis of variance of the judges' ratings was significant ($P < 0.01$), as were the subject's self-ratings ($P < 0.05$).

**Series III–V. Further screening and selected subjects.** Series III was another 12-subject screening device and the overall results were not significant (Ullman, 1969). The most promising subject was selected for Series IV, an eight-night study which also yielded nonsignificant results (Ullman, 1969). In Series V (Krippner, 1969), the second-most promising subject from Series I participated in a sixteen-night study. Unknown to the subject, an agent was present on only eight of the nights. The results were nonsignificant.

**Series VI. Replication with a selected subject.**    The successful subject from Series I–II was again paired with the same agent in an eight-night study (Ullman and Krippner, 1969). The target picture for each session was accompanied by 'multisensory' materials enabling the agent to 'act out' salient aspects of the target (*see* Figures 2.3a and b). The results of this study were highly significant ($P < 0.0001$).

Figure 2.3   (a) Target and (b) multisensory material for the second night of Series VI, 'Downpour at Shono' by Hiroshige (Courtesy, Tudor Publishing Co.). Excerpts from subject's dream reports: 'Something about an Oriental man who was ill . . . it had to do with fountains . . . and a water spray . . .'

**Series VII. Replication with another selected subject.** A subject who had produced significant results in pilot work conducted in another laboratory (Hall, 1967), participated in an eight-night study (Krippner and Ullman, 1970). The subject worked with several different agents, selected on the basis of empathetic response. The results were highly significant ($P < 0.0004$).

**Series VIII. Repeated versus different targets.** Each experiment thus far has involved the use of one target per night. The four subjects in Series VIII (Honorton, Krippner and Ullman, 1972) believed this procedure was in effect, though it was not. In this study, the same target was repeatedly used by the agent over a four-night period, and a different target was used for each dream period over another four-night period. Three of the subjects obtained significantly higher correct-pair ratings in the condition with different targets programmed on a dream-by-dream basis. The fourth subject obtained highly significant overall results ($P < 0.0005$), with no difference between conditions.

**Series IX. Long distance sensory bombardment.** Eight subjects participated one night each while the agent, in another laboratory 14 miles distant, underwent sensory bombardment in an audiovisual chamber (Krippner, et al. 1971). Target programs consisting of thematically related slide sequences (e.g., 'Far Eastern Religions', 'Birth of a Baby') replaced the usual target pictures. The results were statistically significant ($P = 0.004$).

**Series X. Long distance group–agent study.** Two previously successful subjects participated in this study (Krippner, Honorton and Ullman, 1972a) carried out in cooperation with a popular American music group, 'The Grateful Dead'. The group gave a series of six late-evening concerts in Port Chester, N.Y., a distance of approximately 45 miles from the laboratory. On each night, the audience (averaging about 2000) was shown slides with instructions ('You are about to participate in an ESP experiment . . .') followed by a target slide. They were given the name and location of one subject but not the other. Results for the subject identified to the audience were significant ($P = 0.012$), while the subject who was not identified obtained nonsignificant results.

**Telepathy pilot sessions.** Between 1964 and 1969, 83 pilot sessions involving subject–agent pairs were completed (Ullman, Krippner and Honorton, 1970). These exploratory sessions were conducted to screen potentially talented subjects, assess procedural innovations, etc. The experimental controls used in these pilot sessions were the same as for the formal studies. The results were highly significant ($P < 0.00001$).

**Series XI. A precognitive dream study.** A subject with a reported history of ostensible precognitive experiences participated in an eight-night study in which he attempted to dream

Figure 2.4 Sample from target program, 'Birds', used on the sixteenth night of the second precognitive dream study (Series XII). Excerpts from the subject's dreams: '. . . It involved Bob Morris. His experiments with birds . . . A few ducks and things . . . there are quite a lot of mandrake geese and various birds . . . I just have a feeling that the next target material will be about birds.'

about an experience to be randomly determined for him on the following day (Krippner, Ullman and Honorton, 1971). A complex procedure was devised for random determination of the target experience. The results were highly significant ($P = 0.00018$).

**Series XII. Precognitive replication.** The same subject participated in a sixteen-night series (Krippner, Honorton and Ullman, 1972b). On odd-numbered (1, 3, 5 . . . 15) nights, the subject attempted to dream about target programs he would be shown on even-numbered (2, 4, 6 . . . 16) nights. Target programs consisted of sequences of coloured slides and coordinated sound effects structured around a particular theme (e.g., '2001', 'Police', 'Birds', *see* Figure 2.4). Following each precognitive (odd-numbered) night, a staff technician 'blind' to the subject's dream reports, initiated a complex procedure to randomly select a target program. The results were highly significant for the precognitive nights ($P = 0.0012$) but not for the (even-numbered) nights following the experience.

**Survey of other studies.** The above investigations were all conducted in our laboratory at Maimonides Medical Center. Several attempts to replicate these studies have been reported by independent investigators. Globus, *et al.* (1968) conducted a seventeen-night study with one subject who claimed psychic ability. Evaluation of judges' ratings did not yield overall significant results, although sessions which the judges rated with high confidence were significant. Hall (1967) reported significant results in a pilot study with one subject. Belvedere and Foulkes (1971) and Foulkes, *et al.* (1972) reported attempted replications of Maimonides Series VII and IX which yielded nonsignificant results. Van de Castle (1971) reported significant results in an experiment involving spontaneous dream recall.

## ESP AND HYPNOSIS

### State-specific characteristics of hypnosis

Hypnosis as traditionally conceptualised is an artifically induced ASC brought about through certain 'induction' techniques. The basic characteristics attributed to hypnosis include passivity, redistribution of attention, increased fantasy and role behaviour, reduction in reality testing with increased tolerance for reality distortion, and hypersuggestibility (Hilgard, 1965). No physiological correlates have been discovered which reliably distinguish hypnotic and waking states, and recent studies (Barber, 1969) call into question many of the traditional constructs associated with hypnotic behaviour.

### Early claims

Since the time of Mesmer (1734–1815), claims have been made for 'travelling clairvoyance', 'community of sensation', 'suggestion at a distance' and other ostensibly paranormal effects in hypnosis (Dingwall, 1967). In the early part of the nineteenth century, these so-called 'higher phenomena of hypnotism' were widely regarded as a defining characteristic of deep hypnosis (Binet and Féré, 1888).

## Hypnotic *vs* waking card guessing performance

Twelve experimental studies have been reported, comparing ESP card guessing performance in hypnotic and waking states (Honorton and Krippner, 1969). These experiments suggest that hypnosis does affect ESP. Nine of the twelve studies produced significant differences between hypnotic and waking card guessing success. These studies indicate that hypnosis affects ESP magnitude (size of deviation) rather than direction (sign of deviation, above or below chance). Examination of these studies further suggests that hypnotic increments in ESP deviations are not attributable to direct suggestions for high scoring and suggestibility is not, in itself, highly correlated with extrasensory success (Honorton, 1969a; Stanford, 1972).

Several novel approaches involving ESP and hypnosis have been reported and will be briefly summarised.

**Telepathic hypnosis.**  Vasiliev (1963) reported successful confirmation of the nineteenth century claim of 'suggestion at a distance' in experiments involving the hypnotist-agent's attempts to influence subjects' grasp on a rubber bulb at randomly determined intervals. Vasiliev reported only six failures in 260 trials. Unfortunately, these studies have not been described in sufficient detail to allow proper critical assessment.

**Hypnotic discrimination of correct/incorrect responses.** Fahler and Osis (1966) have reported a study with two subjects who under hypnosis were given instructions designed to encourage introspective discrimination between correct and incorrect ESP responses. In 1950 trials, the subjects made 'confidence calls' on trials they believed most likely to involve ESP. The results for confidence call trials were highly significant ($P = 2 \times 10^{-8}$).

**Hypnotic training of ESP?** Considerable interest was aroused by recent claims (Ryzl, 1966) of a hypnotic training technique for the development of ESP in unselected subjects. The technique itself has been summarised elsewhere (Honorton and Krippner, 1969). While one subject who underwent Ryzl's 'training' program has maintained significant scoring levels in an extended series of experiments (Ryzl and Otani, 1967), it is not clear what role, if any, hypnotic preparation played, and a number of unsuccessful attempts to validate the technique have been reported (Stephenson, 1965; Haddox, 1966; Beloff and Mandleberg, 1966). It should be noted, however, that all of the attempted replications reported thus far have deviated from Ryzl's technique in potentially important ways.

**ESP in hypnotically induced dreams.**    Krippner (1968) reported a study of waking, dream, and hypnotic imagery in relation to ESP. Sixteen subjects produced imagery reports while an agent concentrated on randomly selected target pictures. Half of the subjects were hypnotised and half comprised a waking control group. For the hypnosis group, significant target–imagery correspondences were obtained ($P < 0.001$) following a posthypnotic nap. Control subjects obtained significant correspondences ($P < 0.01$) relating to imagery elicited through spontaneous dream recall.

Honorton and Stump (1969) selected six subjects falling in the upper quartile of a standard test of hypnotic susceptibility, for an experiment on hypnotically induced clairvoyant dreams. Following induction of hypnosis, the subjects were given suggestions to dream (while in hypnosis) about randomly selected target pictures enclosed in opaque envelopes. Five subjects completed four hypnotic dreams with four different targets and one subject completed eight hypnotic dreams with eight targets in two sessions. Blind evaluation of target–dream pairs by the subjects yielded significant results ($P < 0.02$), while nonsignificant results were obtained by an outside judge. Examples of the target pictures are shown in Figures 2.5 and 2.6.

A partially successful replication of this study (significant at the $0.02$ level) was reported by Parker and Beloff (1970) in an experiment methodologically very similar except for the inclusion of a second session for each of the ten subjects. A significant decline effect ($P = 0.011$) was found between the two sessions. A second experiment failed to yield significant results. Two additional independent replications yielding significant results have recently been reported (Glick and Kogen, 1971; Keeling, 1971).

A replication and extension of the Honorton–Stump study (Honorton, 1972) yielded significant results ($P < 0.04$) for hypnotic subjects with high susceptibility ratings. Subjects with low susceptibility ratings and subjects in a 'waking imagination' group did not obtain significant results. Self-ratings of 'dream quality' and 'state reports' designed to assess subjects' self-evaluation of hypnotic 'depth' were used as converging measures. High dream quality ratings and state reports were associated with significantly more ESP hits (correct target–transcript pairs).

Figure 2.5   Target from hypnotic dream study, 'The Adoration of the Shepherds' by El Greco (Metropolitan Museum of Art, the H. O. Havermyer Collection). Subject's hypnotic dream report: 'The Virgin Mary. A statue and Jesus Christ. An old church with two pillars overgrown with grass by the church entrance. The Virgin Mary was holding Jesus as a baby'.

## ESP AND ALPHA-RELATED STATES

### State-specific characteristics

EEG alpha rhythm activity (8–13 Hz) most prominent in the occipital cortex has been associated with a state of detached awareness, reduction in cognitive processing, and relaxation (Kamiya, 1968; Brown, 1971). Attempts to parcel out state-specific characteristics from constitutional factors indicate alpha to be associated with an internally directed shift in attention, reduction in eye movement activity (probably related to a decrease in mental imagery), and decreased muscle tonus (Honorton, Davidson and Bindler, 1972). Much of the current interest in alpha states stems from the finding that advanced practitioners of zen and yoga meditation exhibit increases in alpha amplitude and abundance (Kasamatsu and Hirai, 1966; Anand, Chhina and Singh, 1961; Wallace, 1970).

Figure 2.6    Target from hypnotic dream study, 'The Kinryuszan Temple' by
Hiroshige (Courtesy, Tudor Publishing Co.). Subject's hypnotic
dream report: 'A lot of things—a car going by. A room with party
decorations. Thought I saw people but there wasn't anyone there.
Then everything went white. I saw a gold chest, like a pirate's chest,
but shining and new. No decorations on the floor, they were on the
ceiling and walls. There was a table with things on it. Red balloons,
red punch bowls'.

## Alpha-related states and ESP–Anecdotal

From the ancient *Yoga Aphorisms* of Patanjali (Prabhavananda
and Isherwood, 1953) to present times (Yogananda, 1946), states
of consciousness achieved through eastern meditation techniques
have been thought to be associated with concurrent development
of *siddhis*, or paranormal powers. White's (1964) analysis of
introspective reports by 'gifted' subjects suggests a meditative-
type state: ESP receptivity is associated by these subjects with
'deep mental and physical relaxation', reduction of strain, passivity,
withdrawal from the external environment, and ability to 'still' the
mind. These descriptors are also similar to subjective reports by
subjects producing high levels of alpha in the laboratory (Kamiya,
1968; Brown, 1971; Honorton, Davidson and Bindler, 1972).

## Laboratory studies

As a consequence, research exploring various parameters of a possible relationship between ESP and alpha has proliferated rapidly. Over a dozen studies have been reported as of this writing, all but two of which have appeared since 1969. The purpose, methodology, and subject treatment procedures of these studies have varied greatly, as have the types of ESP tasks employed, and a coherent pattern has not as yet emerged from the data. Some of the studies indicate a positive relationship between alpha abundance and ESP (Cadoret, 1964; Honorton, 1969b; Morris and Cohen, 1969; Morris, *et al.*, 1972; Rao and Feola, 1972) while others (Stanford and Lovin, 1970; Honorton and Carbone, 1971) indicate a negative relationship. Still another (Lewis and Schmeidler, 1971) yielded both in the form of a differential relationship with two types of ESP task. The most consistent finding thus far is an ESP related increase in alpha frequency (Stanford and Lovin, 1970; Stanford, 1971; Stanford and Stevenson, 1972).

Inferences from these studies concerning states of consciousness have been based exclusively on EEG criteria. In a recent study involving biofeedback training (Honorton, Davidson and Bindler, 1971), 23 subjects were trained to control alpha production in a series of alternating ON/OFF trials (Kamiya, 1968). In addition to occipital EEG activity, subjects' eye movements and muscle tension levels were monitored. Subjects were instructed to give 'state reports' while attempting to increase (alpha ON) or decrease (alpha OFF) alpha. The state report scale was designed to measure degree of relaxation and directionality of attention (from externalised to internalised). While alpha, eye movements, and muscle tension were not significantly interrelated, state reports were interrelated with all three physiological measures. High state reports (defined as internally directed attention and relaxation) were associated with relatively high alpha and with reduced eye movement and muscle tension activity (Honorton, Davidson and Bindler, 1972), giving construct validity to the state report scale. In a second session, subjects completed clairvoyant card guessing tasks while alternately increasing/decreasing alpha and giving state reports. Subjects with high state reports obtained significantly higher ESP scores ($P < 0·01$) in alpha ON trials and significantly lower scores in alpha OFF trials ($P < 0·01$). This apparent interaction of self-report and EEG measures on ESP suggests that psi is enhanced by the state upon which these measures converge. Further support for this conclusion is evident in a more detailed analysis involving subjects who completely conformed to the expected alpha state pattern (alpha ON/high state reports, alpha OFF/low state reports). These subjects, comprising about half of the total subject sample ($N = 12$) obtained independently significant ($P < 0.01$) above chance scores in alpha-ON trials. As in the hypnotic dream study reviewed above (Honorton, 1972), subjects with large state report shifts toward internally directed attention obtained significantly higher ESP scores than subjects with little or no shift in attention ($P = 0.05$).

Similar results have been obtained in an ESP experiment conducted under conditions of partial sensory isolation (Honorton, Drucker and Hermon, 1973). In this study, subjects gave state reports at five-minute intervals while confined in a free swinging, suspended sensory isolation cradle. During the last ten minutes of confinement, an agent in another room attempted to influence the subject's mental imagery with a randomly selected target picture. Subjects with high state reports obtained a significant level of success ($P = 0.025$). The amount of *shift* in state (from first to last ten-minute periods) was related to success: subjects with strong (above mean) internally oriented shifts obtained significant above chance scoring ($P = 0.011$), while subjects with little (below mean) shift, or externally oriented shifts, obtained nonsignificant below chance scores.

## TENTATIVE GENERALISATIONS AND FUTURE DIRECTIONS

What is the common denominator for the apparent psi enhancing effects of these psychophysiologically heterogeneous ASCs? The difficulties in influencing dream content through sensory stimulation, noted before, attest to the sensory withdrawal characteristic of dreaming; hypnosis involves withdrawal of attention from the external environment, relative to nonhypnotised wakefulness; alpha activity (usually prominent in hypnosis) is blocked by sensory stimulation; and similar effects are produced directly in sensory isolation.

*Empirical generalisation I.* Success in extrasensory tasks will be augmented by attenuation of externally directed attentive activity.

The studies incorporating phenomenological measures (Honorton, Davidson and Bindler, 1971; Honorton, Drucker and Hermon,

1973; Honorton, 1972) indicate that successful psi performance is associated with rapid shifts from one state to another.

*Empirical generalisation 2.* Relatively large and rapid shifts in state will be associated with enhanced ESP performance.

It is not as yet clear whether this proposition should be stated in terms of *directional* shift. Several studies showing significant positive correlations between slower frequency alpha activity in a pretest 'mind clearing' period and subsequent ESP success have also shown significant ESP related acceleration of alpha frequency during the ESP task itself (Stanford and Lovin, 1970; Stanford and Stevenson, 1972). ESP processing may involve several rather distinct phases, with internalised awareness in the preparatory (reception?) phase followed by slight increases in arousal during the response phase.

Such interpretation is consistent with the phenomenological descriptions of apparently gifted subject (White, 1964) and with the 'shutting down' and refocusing ('centring') of attention reported in the meditation literature (e.g., Prabhavananda and Isherwood, 1953). While the investigation of ESP in meditative states is just beginning, preliminary explorations (Osis and Bokert, 1971; Schmeidler, 1970) have been encouraging.

The delineation of psi optimal states on a descriptive level provides the basis for a functional approach in which subjects may be trained (e.g., biofeedback/meditation) to enter and control the states. The Honorton, Davidson and Bindler (1971) study is prototypical of this approach.

## REFERENCES

Anand, B., Chhina, G., and Singh, B. (1961) Some aspects of electroencephalographic studies in yogis. *Electroencephalo. clin. Neurphysiol.*, **13,** 452–456

Barber, T. X. (1969) *Hypnosis: a scientific approach.* Van Nostrand Reinhold, New York

Beloff, J., and Mandleberg, I (1966) 'An attempted validation of the "Ryzl technique" for training ESP subjects.' *J. S.P.R.*, **43,** 229–249

Belvedere, E., and Foulkes, D. (1971) 'Telepathy and dreams: a failure to replicate.' *Percep. mot. Skills*, **33,** 783–789

Binet, A., and Féré, S. (1888) *Animal Magnetism.* Appleton, New York

Boring, E. G. (1953) 'A history of introspection.' *Psych. Bull.*, **50,** 169–189

Brown, B. (1971) 'Awareness of EEG-subjective activity relationships detected within a closed feedback system.' *Psychophysiol.*, **7**, 451–464

Cadoret, R. J. (1964) 'An exploratory experiment: continuous EEG recording during clairvoyant card tests.' *J. Parapsychol.*, **28**, 226. (Abstract)

Devereaux, G. (1953) *Psychoanalysis and the Occult.* International Universities Press, New York

Dingwall, E. J. (Ed.) (1967) *Abnormal Hypnotic Phenomena* (4 Vols), Churchill, London

Fahler, J., and Osis, K. (1966) 'Checking for awareness of hits in a precognition experiment with hypnotized subjects.' *J. Amer. S.P.R.*, **60**, 340–346

Foulkes, D., Belvedere, E., Masters, R., Houston, J., Krippner, S., Honorton, C., and Ullman, M. (1972) 'Long-distance "sensory-bombardment" ESP in dreams: a failure to replicate.' *Percep. mot. Skills*, **35**, 731–734

Galton, F. (1883) *Inquiries into Human Faculties.* Longmans, London

Garner, W. R., Hake, H., and Ericksen, C. W. (1956) 'Operationism and the concept of perception.' *Psychol. Rev.*, **63**, 149–159

Glick, B., and Kogen, J. (1971) 'Clairvoyance in hypnotized subjects: positive results.' *J. Parapsychol.*, **35**, 331. (Abstract)

Globus, G. (1968) 'An appraisal of telepathic communication in dreams.' *Psychophysiol.*, **4**, 365. (Abstract)

Haddox, V. (1966) 'A pilot study of a hypnotic method for training subjects in ESP.' *J. Parapsychol.*, **30**, 277–278. (Abstract)

Hall, C. (1967) (Experiments with telepathically influenced dreams.) *Zeitschrift fur Parapsychologie und Grenzgebiete der Psychologie*, **10**, 18–47

Hartmann, E. (1967) *The Biology of Dreaming.* C. C. Thomas, Springfield, Ill.

Hilgard, E. (1965) *Hypnotic Susceptibility.* Harcourt, Brace & World, New York

Hilgard, E. (1969) 'Altered states of awareness.' *J. Nerv. ment. Dis.*, **149**, 68–79

Honorton, C. (1969a) 'A combination of techniques for the separation of high- and low-scoring ESP subjects: experiments with hypnotic and waking-imagination instructions.' *J. Amer. S.P.R.*, **63**, 69–82

Honorton, C. (1969b) 'Relationship between EEG alpha activity and ESP card-guessing performance.' *J. Amer. S.P.R.*, **63**, 365–374

Honorton, C. (1972) 'Significant factors in hypnotically-induced clairvoyant dreams.' *J. Amer. S.P.R.*, **66**, 86–102

Honorton, C., and Carbone, M. (1971) 'A preliminary study of feedback-augmented EEG alpha activity and ESP card-guessing performance.' *J. Amer. S.P.R.*, **65**, 66–74

Honorton, C., Davidson, R., and Bindler, P. (1971) 'Feedback-augmented EEG alpha, shifts in subjective state, and ESP card-guessing performance.' *J. Amer. S.P.R.*, **65**, 308–323

Honorton, C., Davidson, R., and Bindler, P. (1972) 'Shifts in subjective state associated with feedback-augmented EEG alpha.' *Psychophysiol.*, **9**, 269–270. (Abstract)

Honorton, C., Drucker, S., and Hermon, H. (in press) 'Shifts in subjective state and ESP under conditions of partial sensory deprivation.' *J. Amer. S.P.R.*

Honorton, C., Drucker, S., and Hermon, H. (1973) 'Shifts in subjective state and ESP under conditions of partial sensory deprivation.' *J. Amer. S.P.R.*, **67**, 191–197

Honorton, C., Krippner, S., and Ullman, M. (1971) 'Telepathic transmission of art prints under two conditions.' *Proc. 80th ann. conv. Amer. Psychol. Assn.*, 319–320

Honorton, C., and Stump, J. (1969) 'A preliminary study of hypnotically-induced clairvoyant dreams.' *J. Amer. S.P.R.*, **63**, 175–184

Kamiya, J. (1969) 'Operant control of the EEG alpha rhythm and some of its reported effects on consciousness.' In C. Tart (Ed.) *Altered States of Consciousness*. Wiley, New York.

Kasamatsu, A., and Hirai, T. (1966) 'An electroencephalographic study of the zen meditation (zazen).' *Folia Psychiatrica et Neurologica Japonica*, **20**, 315–336

Keeling, K. (1971) 'Telepathic transmission in hypnotic dreams: an exploratory study.' *J. Parapsychol.*, **35**, 330–331

Krippner, S. (1968) 'Experimentally-induced telepathic effects in hypnosis and non-hypnosis groups.' *J. Amer. S.P.R.*, **62**, 387–398

Krippner, S. (1969) 'Investigations of "extra-sensory" phenomena in dreams and other altered states of consciousness.' *J. Amer. Soc. psychosom. dent. Med.*, **16**, 7–14

Krippner, S., Honorton, C., and Ullman, M. (1972a) 'A long-distance ESP dream study with the "Grateful Dead." ' *J. Amer. Soc. psychosom. dent. Med.*, **19**, in press

Krippner, S., Honorton, C., and Ullman, M. (1972b) A second precognitive dream study with Malcolm Bessent. *J. A.S.P.R.*, **66**, 269–279

Krippner, S., Honorton, C., Ullman, M., Masters, R., and Houston, J. (1971) 'A long-distance "sensory-bombardment" study of ESP in dreams.' *J. Amer. S.P.R.*, **65**, 468–475

Krippner, S., and Ullman, M. (1970) 'Telepathy and dreams: a controlled experiment with EEG-EOG monitoring.' *J. Nerv. ment. Dis.*, **151**, 394–403

Krippner, S., Ullman, M., and Honorton, C. (1971) 'A precognitive dream study with a single subject.' *J. Amer. S.P.R.*, **65**, 192–203

Lewis, L., and Schmeidler, G. (1971) 'Alpha relations with non-intentional and purposeful ESP after feedback.' *J. A.S.P.R.*, **65**, 455–467

Ludwig, A. (1966) 'Altered states of consciousness.' *Arch. gen. Psychiat.*, **15**, 225–234

Miller, N. (1959) 'Liberalization of basic S-R concepts: Extensions to conflict behavior, motivation and social learning.' In S. Koch (Ed.) *Psychology: a study of a science*, Vol. 2, 196–292. McGraw-Hill, New York

Morris, R., and Cohen, D. (1969) 'A preliminary experiment on the relationships among ESP, alpha rhythm, and calling patterns.' *J. Parapsychol.*, **33**, 341. (Abstract)

Morris, R., Roll, W. G., Klein, J., and Wheeler, G. (1972) 'EEG patterns and ESP results in forced-choice experiments with Lalsingh Harribance.' *J. A.S.P.R.*, **66**, 253–268

Myers, F. W. H. (1902) *Human Personality and its Survival of Bodily Death* (2 Vol.). Longmans, London

Osis, K., and Bokert, E. (1971) 'ESP and changed states of consciousness induced by meditation.' *J. Amer. S.P.R.*, **65**, 17–65

Parker, A., and Beloff, J. (1970) 'Hypnotically-induced clairvoyant dreams: a partial replication and attempted confirmation.' *J. Amer. S.P.R.*, **64**, 432–442

Prabhavananda, S., and Isherwood, C. (1953) *How to Know God: the yoga aphorisms of Patanjali.* New American Library, New York

Rao, K. R., and Feola, J. (1972) 'Alpha rhythm and ESP in a free response situation.' *J. Parapsychol.*, **36**, in press. (Abstract)

Rhine, J. B. (1934) *Extrasensory Perception.* Boston: Humphries

Rhine, L. E. (1962) 'Psychological processes in ESP experiences. I. Waking experiences.' *J. Parapsychol.*, **26**, 88–111

Ryzl, M. (1966) 'A method of training in ESP.' *Int. J. Parapsychol.*, **8**, 501–532

Ryzl, M., and Otani, S. (1967) 'An experiment in duplicate calling with Stepanek.' *J. Parapsychol.*, **31**, 19–28

Schmeidler, G. (1970) 'High ESP scores after a Swami's brief instruction in meditation and breathing.' *J. Amer. S.P.R.*, **64**, 100–103

Stanford, R. G. (1971) 'EEG alpha activity and ESP performance: a replicative study.' *J. Amer. S.P.R.*, **65**, 144–154

Stanford, R. G. (1972) 'Suggestibility and success at augury—

divination from "chance" outcomes.' *J. Amer. S.P.R.*, **66,** 42–62

Stanford, R. G. and Lovin, C. (1970) 'EEG alpha activity and ESP performance.' *J. Amer. S.P.R.*, **64,** 375–384

Stanford, R. G., and Stevenson, I. (1972) 'EEG correlates of free-response GESP in an individual subject.' *J. Amer. S.P.R.*, **66,** 357–368

Stephenson, C. J. (1965) 'Cambridge ESP-hypnosis experiments (1958–64).' *J. S.P.R.*, **43,** 77–91

Stoyva, J., and Kamiya, J. (1968) 'Electrophysiological studies of dreaming as the prototype of a new strategy in the study of consciousness.' *Psychol. Rev.*, **75,** 192–205

Tart, C. T. (1965) 'Toward the experimental control of dreaming: a review of the literature.' *Psych. Bull.*, **64,** 81–91

Tart, C. T. (Ed.) (1969) *Altered states of consciousness.* Wiley, New York

Ullman, M. (1969) 'Telepathy and dreams.' *Exper. Med. and Surg.*, **27,** 19–38

Ullman, M., and Krippner, S. (1969) 'A laboratory approach to the nocturnal dimension of paranormal experience: report of a confirmatory study using the REM monitoring technique.' *Bio. Psychiat.*, **1,** 259–270

Ullman, M., and Krippner, S. (1970) *Dream Studies and Telepathy.* Parapsych. Monogr. No. 12, New York: Parapsychology Foundation

Ullman, M., Krippner, S., and Feldstein, S. (1966) 'Experimentally induced telepathic dreams: two studies using EEG-REM monitoring technique.' *Int. J. Neuropsychiat.*, **2,** 420–437

Ullman, M., Krippner, S., and Honorton, C. (1970) 'A review of the Maimonides dream ESP experiments: 1964–1969.' *Psychophysiol.*, **7,** 352–353. (Abstract)

Van de Castle, R. L. (1971) 'The study of GESP in a group setting by means of dreams.' *J. Parapsychol.*, **35,** 312. (Abstract)

Vasiliev, L. L. (1963) *Experiments in Mental Suggestion.* Institute for the Study of Mental Images, Church Crookham, England

Wallace, R. K. (1970) 'Physiological effects of Transcendental Meditation.' *Science*, **222,** 1751–1754

White, R. A. (1964) 'A comparison of old and new methods of response to targets in ESP experiments.' *J. Amer. S.P.R.*, **58,** 21–56

Yogananda (1946) *Autobiography of a Yogi.* Harpers, New York

# 3 Psi and Personality

## K. R. RAO

## SYNOPSIS

The well known work of Gertrude Schmeidler of City College, New York, during the 1950s, can be seen in retrospect as one of the turning points of modern parapsychology. And this for two reasons. In the first place, it sought to bring parapsychology within the ambit of personality theory and hence of general psychology. In the second place it drew attention to the fact that below chance scoring, if significant, could be just as interesting and important as above chance scoring. Although her original 'sheep/goat hypothesis' has not withstood too well the test of time and was certainly not the answer to the repeatability problem as might have been hoped, this is hardly surprising when, as the author puts it, 'belief or disbelief in ESP cannot be a stable feature of any individual. It says very little about the personality of the subject or even his mental state at the time of testing'. Nevertheless, her work began the search for differential scoring effects between contrasted groups which has occupied parapsychologists ever since and to which the author has himself made many valuable contributions.

The author, a psychologist who acquired his parapsychological expertise under J. B. Rhine and now heads a department of psychology and parapsychology at Andhra University, India, here reviews various attempts to link ESP scoring patterns with measures of personality and attitude. The weakness of many previous studies, the author believes, was that they assumed that ESP performance must be a function of one or another personality variable whereas it could be a function of a number of interacting factors. In the past few years, Kanthamani, working under the author, has been investigating the possibility that a combined personality measure based on a number of separate factor scores might provide a better predictor of scoring potential than any of them singly. Using Cattell's HSPQ (a 14-factor personality questionnaire designed for high school children) she took, to start with, the four Cattell factors that correlated best with the children's ESP scores and combined them into a single *measure. As can be seen from Table 3.1, subjects high on this composite scale tended to score above chance while those low on this scale tended to score below chance. Moreover, she found that this combined measure was a better discriminator than any of its component measures alone.*

*Next, she took another set of the Cattell factors to produce a composite 'neuroticism' scale. As can be seen from Table 3.2, this proved an even more successful discriminator, a high score on neuroticism tending to go with psi missing, a low score on neuroticism with psi hitting. A similar compounding of factor scores, using another set of factors from the HSPQ, produced a composite 'extraversion' scale. From Table 3.3 it can be seen that, in general, the extravert is the psi hitter, the introvert the psi misser. This is in line with other studies which the author here surveys.*

*The consistency of the results from these recent Kanthamani and Rao investigations, which cover three confirmatory experiments with different groups of subjects following an initial pilot study, is very promising. Perhaps the day may not be far off when every parapsychologist will have at his disposal a dependable battery of assorted personality and attitude tests on the basis of which he will be able to make his diagnosis and predict, with some degree of confidence, whether his subject is more likely to score above chance, below chance or just at chance.*

*Editor*

One method of studying the relationship between ESP and the personality characteristics of the subject is to enquire into the personality patterns of the outstanding ESP subjects. This has not been found very profitable so far, because several of the studies with outstanding subjects in the past did not involve objective personality assessment. The few available reports seem to indicate more the experimenters' own subjective notions on the possible relationships than a dependable assessment based on objective studies.

The literature on the relationship between ESP and personality factors based on the studies involving unselected subjects is vast and impressive. Yet, if one attempts to sort out methodologically sound and significant studies in this area and draw convincing conclusions on the nature of the relationship, one would not find this task easy. The reasons for this state of affairs are many and varied. In the first place, confirmations of a finding are often lacking. Contradictory findings are not uncommon. Some of the studies, which seem impressive at the outset, lack methodological rigour. It is likely that the confusion in part is due to the legendary elusiveness of psi phenomena and in part to the confounding of variables.

One also suspects that the attempts to explore the relationships between certain personality factors and ESP have rarely proceeded in a systematic and comprehensive fashion. The exception to this is of course the pioneering researches of Gertrude Schmeidler (1958). Her studies of the relationship between subject's belief and disbelief in ESP and his rate of ESP scoring, ranging over a number of years and involving more than a thousand subjects are perhaps the most consistent so far in ESP research.

Schmeidler, in a series of experiments, divided her subjects into two groups, sheep and goats. The sheep were subjects who believed in the possibility of psi, whereas the goats were those who rejected such a possibility. In the individual as well as in group tests, the sheep scored at a significantly higher rate than the goats. In the group tests for example 1157 subjects made 250 875 ESP card trials. The sheep scored at a rate of 5·10 hits per run of 25 trials and the goats obtained an average of 4·93 hits per run. The difference in the rate of scoring between sheep and goats though small enough in absolute terms is highly significant statistically.

The sheep–goat dichotomy was made use of in a number of other studies to separate the hitting and missing subjects. One of the most successful replications of the Schmeidler's study is that of Bhadra (1966), who found that the sheep did significantly better in tests involving ESP symbols. There are, however, some studies (Adcock and Quartermain, 1959; Bevan, 1947) where the sheep–goat dichotomy did not work. There are also some studies where goats did better than the sheep. For example, in a study by Beloff and Bate (1970), it was found that the subjects classified as super-sheep (those who believed in ESP and have confidence in themselves to score high on an ESP task) obtained significantly lower scores than the other groups of subjects.

There are two viewpoints regarding the possible interrelation between personality factors and ESP. Based largely on the lack of consistency in the findings on the relationship between ESP and personality factors Rao (1966) argued that there may not be any intrinsic relationship between personality traits and ESP. People with certain dispositions may do better under one set of circumstances rather than another. The standardised testing procedures that are currently used in ESP research may favour subjects with certain personality characteristics as against their opposites. Eysenck (1967) takes issue with this line of thinking and argues in favour of a theory that assumes a greater intrinsic relationship. Accepting the view that psi is 'an ancient and primitive form of perception' and therefore conditions of high cortical arousal are unfavourable to it, Eysenck goes on to deduce the hypothesis that extraverts would do better than introverts on psi tests because, the introverts habitually are in a state of greater cortical arousal than extraverts. Indeed, there is evidence to show that extraverts do better than introverts in ESP tests. This will be further discussed later in this chapter.

Several studies have shown that a number of personality factors correlate with ESP. But the correlations have been found to be too small to carry much conviction. It would indeed be of interest to see whether by combining factors known to be related to ESP, we would achieve better results than we would by using single factors alone. For some reason this idea has not received the attention it deserved until recently. The promise that a combination of several factors might be more fruitful than single factors is present in the past work. Smith and Humphrey (1946) found, for example, that neither the expansive–compressive ratings nor the scores on the Maslow security–insecurity inventory separated the hitting and missing subjects successfully. When these two measures are combined, they reported, the expansive–secure subjects obtained significantly more hits than the compressive–insecure subjects. That a similar combination of personality measures would be successful is indicated in a study by Stuart (1947) and also in another by McMahan (1946).

Using Stuart's interest inventory scores along with her expansive–compressive ratings, Humphrey (1950) derived another combination of measures. Applying Stuart's criterion of classifying the subjects as 'midrange' and 'extreme' on the interest inventory, Humphrey found that the former group obtained an average of 5·15 hits per run and the latter, 4·81 hits per run. The expansive–compressive breakdown for the same subjects did not give significant results, even though the expansives scored above chance and the compressives below chance. When the data were analysed further by combining both the interest and expansive–compressive ratings, the highest average score was obtained by the expansive–midrange subjects (5·28 hits per run) and the lowest by the compressive–extreme subjects (4·76 hits per run). The difference between these two groups is greater than either of the single measures used separately.

Later, Humphrey (1950) found a new method of classifying the subjects by the interest inventory. She derived a short form of this scale which consisted of fourteen items. The subjects were divided into high and low groups on the basis of the new scale. The high group consisted of those subjects who made eight or more points on the fourteen-item scale, and they were expected to get positive ESP scores. The low group consisted of those subjects who obtained fewer than eight points on the interest scale, and they were expected to score either negatively or at chance in the ESP test. Accordingly, she found that the high subjects obtained an average score of 5·19 hits per run, and the low subjects scored 4·83 hits. The same subjects classified as 'midrange' and 'extreme' on Stuart's full scale interest inventory also gave significant differences. The 'midrange' subjects scored above MCE, the 'extreme' subjects scored less than MCE. When both interest scales were combined, the midrange–high subjects obtained 5·47 hits per run. The difference between these groups was highly significant.

The expansive–compressive breakdown for these subjects did not yield significant results. Adding the expansive–compressive criterion to the former two, a triple combination of personality measures was obtained. The ESP scores of the expansives who were also midrange and high on the interest scales averaged above chance (5·52 hits per run), and those of the compressives who were extreme and low are below chance (4·61 hits per run). The difference between these two groups in their ESP scoring rate was significant. Although this difference is smaller than the one obtained by the combination of the two interest measures, the difference in the average scores for the triple combination are higher than those obtained from any other combination.

Nicol and Humphrey (1953), using a battery of personality questionnaires, derived a combination of two personality traits, namely, selfconfidence as measured by the Guilford-Martin inventory and emotional stability as measured by the Cattell's 16 PF. While both these traits correlated with ESP scores to a significant degree their combined effect was even greater. The correlation between ESP scores and selfconfidence was found to be $+0·55$ and with emotional stability it was $+0·47$. To see the combined effect of the two measures together, the multiple correlation technique was used. The obtained correlation between selfconfidence plus emotional stability and ESP score was 0·65, which is highly significant. Nicol and Humphrey pointed out that the use of two measures together, even after their intercorrelation was removed, gave a better account of the experimental results than either measure used separately.

Schmeidler's extensive work (1950b, 1960) with Rorschach, along with her studies relating to attitudes and ESP, provides further evidence in support of the efficacy of combined personality measures in separating the high and low scoring subjects. Schmeidler obtained significant differences between sheep and goats. Further, the sheep–goat difference was more pronounced with the well adjusted subjects than with the poorly adjusted ones. The well adjusted sheep obtained higher average scores on the ESP test than sheep in general, and the well adjusted goats obtained lower average scores than the goats in general.

In her pooled data of 27 group experiments the following results were obtained. The average score of all sheep ($N = 334$) was 5·10 and for all goats ($N = 245$), 4·95. When the adjustment criterion was added to this sheep–goat differentiation, the well adjusted sheep obtained an average of 5·17 hits per run and the well adjusted goats gave an average score of 4·85 hits per run. The adjustment criterion alone did not give a significant breakdown with the ESP scores, but when combined with the sheep–goat differentiation, a highly significant breakdown between well adjusted sheep and well adjusted goats was obtained. The differences between poorly adjusted sheep and goats were insignificant.

Schmeidler (1952b) reports another study in which she used the Allport-Vernon Study of Values (AVSV) along with the sheep-goat classification. She found that when the scores on the theoretical value system of the AVSV were combined with the attitude ratings, greater differentiation in the ESP scores of sheep and goats was noticed than when either of the measures was used alone. The sheep–goat differentiation for 63 subjects who participated in this experiment was significant. The sheep obtained an average of 5·30 and the goats 4·93 hits per run. When the subjects were divided into theoretical and nontheoretical on the basis of AVSV ratings, the former group scored 5·31 hits per run and the latter 5·09 hits per run. The difference between the two groups, however, was insignificant. When the value ratings and the sheep–goat classification were combined, the average of the theoretical sheep rose to 5·68 hits per run and that of theoretical goats came down to 4·85.

In the studies reported above, except the card series in Stuart's study (1947), a greater separation between hitting and missing was obtained when combined measures were used than when single measures were employed. This fact was recognised by Mangan (1958) when he reviewed several such studies and observed that the expression of ESP is influenced by a number of personality factors working in combination.

No systematic efforts were made to exploit this possibility of achieving a more reliable prediction of subject's performance in ESP tests, until Kanthamani (Kanthamani and Rao, 1971, 1972a, 1972b, 1973) took up her studies of the personality characteristics of ESP subjects. In a series of four experimental studies she attempted to isolate the primary personality factors which are related to ESP performance. She then sought to combine the relevant factors to see whether the combined personality measure (CPM) would provide a better separation of hitting and missing subjects. I shall now deal with her work in some detail as I consider it to be among the most important to date.

In a pilot test and three other confirmatory experiments, Kanthamani studied a total of 146 boys and girls of age range 16 to 18 years, studying in English medium schools and a junior college in India. She administered an eight run ESP test to each subject individually in two different sessions using the standard ESP cards with the blind matching technique. She also gave her young adolescent subjects Cattell's high school personality questionnaire (HSPQ) to assess both the primary characteristics and the broader dimensions of their personality.

Among the 14 primary personality factors measured by the HSPQ, she found only four factors (A, E, F and I, 'cyclothmyia', 'dominance', 'surgency' and 'harria' respectively) to be significantly related to their ESP scoring.

The warm and sociable subjects (A+) scored higher on the ESP test than those rated as critical and aloof (A−). Subjects who were more dominant (E+) scored positively on ESP and those who were submissive (E−) scored negatively. Happy-go-lucky subjects (F+) scored positively and serious minded subjects (F−) negatively. Tough, realistic subjects (I+) scored positively and aesthetically sensitive ones (I−) scored negatively.

She further tried a combination of these successful factors (A, E, F, I) to differentiate the subjects. The combined personality measure (CPM), a combination of the above four personality factors, represents a broader dimension of the subject's personality. She divided her subjects into two groups, the low CPM group and high CPM group, taking the theoretical mean as the cutting point. The low CPM group and the high CPM group were compared for their ESP test performance. The scores of the high CPM and low CPM groups are given in Table 3.1. The High CPM subjects obtained more hits than the low CPM subjects, the difference between the two groups being significant in all the four experiments. The CPM provided a better separation of hitting and missing subjects than any of the four primary factors taken individually. Her studies thus lead us to the conclusion that the

TABLE 3.1   Combined personality measure (CPM) and ESP Score

| Experiment | LOW CPM | | | | |
| | No. of subjects | Runs | Hits | Deviation | Mean run score |
| --- | --- | --- | --- | --- | --- |
| Pilot | 8 | 64 | 263 | −57 | 4·11 |
| Confirmatory Experiment 1 | 24 | 192 | 879 | −81 | 4·58 |
| Confirmatory Experiment 2 | 20 | 160 | 789 | −11 | 4·93 |
| Confirmatory Experiment 3 | 21 | 168 | 751 | −89 | 4·47 |

| Experiment | HIGH CPM | | | | |
| | No. of subjects | Runs | Hits | Deviation | Mean run score |
| --- | --- | --- | --- | --- | --- |
| Pilot | 14 | 112 | 627 | +67 | 5·60 |
| Confirmatory Experiment 1 | 26 | 208 | 1096 | +56 | 5·27 |
| Confirmatory Experiment 2 | 16 | 128 | 692 | +52 | 5·41 |
| Confirmatory Experiment 3 | 17 | 136 | 659 | −21 | 4·85 |

primary personality factors are able to separate psi hitters and psi missers better when working jointly rather than individually.

The subject high on CPM, who may be expected to give positive scores in an ESP test, is one who is warm and sociable rather than aloof and stiff, good natured and easy going rather than critical and suspicious. At the same time he is assertive and self-assured rather than submissive and dependent. He is tough and less easily upset; he is enthusiastic, talkative, cheerful, quick and alert. He tends to be adventurous, impulsive, emotional, and care-free, but he is also realistic and composed. It is the combination of these factors that seem to make the subject a positive scorer.

The psi missing subject gives just the opposite pattern. He tends to be tense, excitable and frustrated. He is demanding, impatient, dependent and sensitive. He is also timid, threat-sensitive, shy, and withdrawn. Other characteristics of the psi misser are sub-missiveness, suspicion and depression-proneness.

While it is of considerable interest to note that the CPM worked better than any of the primary personality factors in separating hitters and missers, Kanthamani found that the neuroticism dimension is about the most effective in separating her hitting and missing subjects. She divided her subjects into high $N$ and low $N$ groups taking the theoretical mean of 22 as the dividing point. The two groups thus formed were compared in respect to their ESP scores using a $t$ test. In the pilot experiment the low $N$ group averaged 5·64 hits per run and the high $N$ obtained an average of 4·03. The ESP score of low $N$ group is significantly better than the high $N$ group. As may be seen from Table 3.2 a similar tendency of low $N$ subjects to score at a higher rate than the high $N$ subjects is apparent in the confirmatory experiments. Thus the results indicate a fairly strong relationship between ESP scoring level and neuroticism scores obtained through the HSPQ.

There is of course evidence in previous literature to suggest this relationship. For example, adjustment level, frustration tolerance, stress tolerance and anxiety, which are indirect measures of neurotic tendency, appear to have relevance to an individual's psi ability.

Kahn (1952) found that the subjects who were above average in personal adjustment scored positively and those who were below average scored negatively in ESP tests. The adjustment level of

TABLE 3.2  ESP scores in relation to the N-scale (Neuroticism)

| Experiment | Groups | No. of subjects | Runs | Devia-tion | Mean hits per run |
|---|---|---|---|---|---|
| Pilot | Low *N* | 14 | 112 | +72 | 5·64 |
| | High *N* | 8 | 64 | −62 | 4·03 |
| Confirmatory Experiment 1 | Low *N* | 29 | 232 | +73 | 5·32 |
| | High *N* | 21 | 168 | −98 | 4·42 |
| Confirmatory Experiment 2 | Low *N* | 15 | 120 | +68 | 5·57 |
| | High *N* | 21 | 168 | −27 | 4·84 |
| Confirmatory Experiment 3 | Low *N* | 19 | 152 | −22 | 4·86 |
| | High *N* | 19 | 152 | −88 | 4·42 |

his subjects was obtained by using the Heston personal adjustment inventory.

The subjects classified as secure and insecure showed a similar trend in two studies, one by Smith and Humphrey (1946) and the other by Stuart and others (1947). In both the studies they used the Maslow security–insecurity inventory and found that the secure subjects tended to score higher in an ESP test than the insecure subjects.

Rivers (1950), who administered clairvoyance and GESP tests to a group of high school and college students along with the mental health analysis test, found that those who were rated as showing relatively marked 'behavioural immaturity', 'emotional instability', and 'feelings of inadequacy' among the high school subjects obtained higher scores on the clairvoyance tests than those who were relatively free of these characteristics. But there was only a slight relationship between these characteristics and GESP scores. Among the college students none of the ratings showed any relationship with their ESP test performance.

This apparently contradictory nature of River's findings indicates the possible interaction of certain other factors like the subject's attitude, etc.

Using a projective test Eilbert and Schmeidler (1950) and Schmeidler (1950a) studied the frustration tolerance side of the neuroticism dimension. The picture frustration test (PF) rated the subjects as to their direction of aggression in frustration arousing situations into one of the following three categories:

1. extrapunitives, who tend to blame the source of frustration,
2. intropunitives, who tend to blame themselves and
3. impunitives, who tend to treat the situation impersonally.

The results showed a negative correlation between ESP scores and extrapunitiveness and a positive correlation between ESP and impunitiveness.

In another study by Schmeidler (1954), the correlations between PF ratings and ESP scores were low and insignificant, though they were in the expected direction. However, when only the moderately frustrated subjects were analysed the correlation increased to a significant degree suggesting that the variable involved here is adjustment. Both extrapunitives, who direct their aggression towards the source of frustration and intropunitives who direct their aggression towards themselves tend to be more poorly adjusted than impunitives.

Neurotic disposition measured through the defence mechanism test (DMT) was also found to be related to ESP. Carpenter (1965) and Johnson and Kanthamani (1967) found that the subjects who were rated as showing low defences, indicating good adjustment, tended to score positively while those who were rated as showing high defences, indicating poor adjustment, tended to score negatively in ESP tests.

The study of anxiety, a more important component of neuroticism, was attempted by Rao (1965a) and Freeman and Nielsen (1964) using the Taylor's Manifest Anxiety Scale (MAS) and the ESP scores. But, Rao's finding that low anxious would do better in an ESP task than high anxious subjects was not the same as the one by Freeman and Nielsen, who found their high anxious subjects scoring the highest, low anxious next best and mid-anxious the least. Since the ESP tests employed by these investigators were different, it was suggested that Rao's test was more difficult than the one administered by Freeman and Nielsen and that the low anxious subjects therefore did better than the high anxious.

Honorton (1965) attempted to test this hypothesis. He used two types of ESP tests involving simple and complex tasks. The high anxious subjects showed a tendency to score above chance in those tests they believed to be simple and at or below chance in the tests they considered complex, though the obtained deviations were not significant.

Several other personality factors that could be considered as related to neuroticism, were found to show a significant relationship with ESP scores. Nicol and Humphrey (1953) used a battery of personality questionnaires that include Guilford's inventory, the Guilford-Martin questionnaire and Cattell's 16 PF. The factors that were positively correlated with ESP scoring are freedom from depression, happy-go-lucky disposition, freedom from nervous tension, emotional stability, calm trustfulness and low irritability level.

The direct measure of neuroticism using the Maudsley personality inventory (MPI) by Astrom (1965) and Green (1966a and 1966b) failed to predict ESP scores.

In addition to the CPM and neuroticism dimensions, Kanthamani also analysed her subjects' psi ability in relation to extraversion.

A combination of the weighted scores on factors A, F, H and $Q_2$ (A, Cyclothymia; F. Surgency; H. Parmia; $Q_2$, Lack of self confidence) gave the extraversion dimension. Taking the theoretical mean as the cutting point, she divided her subjects into two groups —extraverts, and introverts. Table 3.3 shows the ESP results of these two groups. In the pilot experiment the average run scores for the extravert and introvert groups were 5·45 and 4·37 hits respectively. In all the confirmatory experiments the extraverts scored higher than the introverts and the combined evidence

TABLE 3.3   ESP scores in relation to E-Scale (Extraversion)

| Experiment | Groups | No. of subjects | Runs | Deviation | Mean hits per run |
|---|---|---|---|---|---|
| Pilot | Extraverts | 14 | 112 | +50 | 5·45 |
|  | Introverts | 8 | 64 | −40 | 4·37 |
| Confirmatory Experiment 1 | Extraverts | 19 | 152 | +20 | 5·13 |
|  | Introverts | 31 | 248 | −45 | 4·82 |
| Confirmatory Experiment 2 | Extraverts | 17 | 136 | +64 | 5·47 |
|  | Introverts | 19 | 152 | −23 | 4·85 |
| Confirmatory Experiment 3 | Extraverts | 14 | 112 | −6 | 4·95 |
|  | Introverts | 24 | 192 | −104 | 4·46 |

clearly suggests that extraverts tend to score better on psi tests than introverts.

Kanthamani's finding is a confirmation of several studies which indicated a similar relationship. In one attempt, using the Bernreuter Personality Inventory, Humphrey (1945) failed to obtain a significant relationship between extraversion-introversion scores and ESP. But, in a latter attempt (1951) she found in three series of experiments, over 70% of her extravert subjects scored positively in ESP tests while over 70% of the introverts scored negatively. In a replication by Casper (1952) the findings of Humphrey were confirmed. Astrom (1965) using the Maudsley Personality Inventory found that the subjects who scored high on the extraversion scale, obtained an average of 6·65 hits per run and the introverts 4·80 hits per run. The difference between extraverts and introverts was highly significant. However, Green (1966a, 1966b) did not obtain any significant results using the same inventory.

Nicol and Humphrey (1953) using Guilford's STDCR inventory, which gave information about the factors that are generally considered to be the various aspects of extraversion and introversion, namely, social extraversion–introversion, thinking extraversion-introversion, depression, cycloid depression and rhathymia (or happy-go-lucky type), found a suggestive relationship of these factors to ESP. Some of the correlations were very significant while some others in general indicated only a weak relationship.

Nash (1966) used the MMPI in his work with college students. The negative correlation he obtained between ESP and social introversion of his subjects indicates that those who are more introverted obtain lower scores on ESP test than those who are less introverted.

Eysenck (1967) reported a similar study by Black, in which a negative relationship was found between MMPI scores on social introversion and ESP.

Sociability, being one of the most common characteristics of extraversion, is found to be related to ESP among children, in a study by Shields (1962). In her work, the children were classified as 'withdrawn' or 'not withdrawn'. In two experiments using different ESP tests, she found that the 'withdrawn children' scored below chance and the 'not withdrawn' children scored above chance with a significant difference between them.

Van de Castle (1958) studied spontaneity, a characteristic of extraverts using Rorschach in his psychokinetic experiments. The results show a positive relationship between high spontaneity and psychokinesis. In a study by Eilbert and Schmeidler (1950) work habits, like ego involvement and task orientation are found to be related to ESP. They found that the subjects rated as ego involved scored generally below chance while those rated as task oriented tended to score above chance, with a significant difference in between.

Selfconfidence, a characteristic of extraverts, is also found to be positively related to ESP scoring in a study by Nicol and Humphrey (1953), where they used the Guilford-Martin Inventory to obtain selfconfidence scores.

Nash and Nash (1967) found that general activity, which is a characteristic of extraverts, is related to subject's ESP scoring.

From the preceding discussions three conclusions seem to emerge:

1. the subject's belief or disbelief in the possibility of psi is related to his performance on ESP tasks,
2. extraversion and neuroticism dimensions of personality are related to psi,
3. a combination of personality factors seem to predict the direction of a subject's ESP scoring more reliably than any of them taken alone.

Belief or disbelief in ESP cannot be a stable feature of any individual. It says very little about the personality of the subject or even his mental state at the time of the testing. The sceptic, when better informed, may become a believer, and one may be a sheep or a goat for a variety of reasons. It may seem, however, that motivation is at the root of the differential scoring by sheep and goat. The believers generally tended to obtain positive deviations because they as believers were likely to have been motivated to obtain higher scores. The nonbelievers tended to produce negative deviations because their motivation was likely to be in the negative direction. Just as some persons who have strong inhibitions and repressions about certain things tend to fail consistently to recall them, a person who is convinced of the impossibility of psi may develop analogous inhibitions that may cause psi missing.

That extraversion and neuroticism are related to psi cannot be questioned, but the rationale that underlies the relationship is not always clear. A person with relatively low neurotic tendency psi hits while his counterpart with a relatively high neurotic tendency psi misses. There is no good sense in which we can say that the former has more ESP than the latter. Psi missing and psi hitting do not differ in their evidential value. If, then, the extravert as well as the introvert, the subject with high neurotic tendency and the one with low neurotic tendency have ESP which works in opposite directions it becomes less feasible to suppose that there is any intrinsic relationship between psi and personality factors. The reason why an extravert does better than an introvert may be found in their differential reaction to the testing situation. This reaction is likely to be psychological and motivational rather than physiological. If one is a firm believer in the physiological basis of personality it would be worthwhile to extend the scope of one's explorations into the physiological realm of psi. Until acceptable correlations between a subject's physiological states and his ESP scoring are obtained, the evidence is very much in favour of a psychological interpretation.

The fact that combined personality measures have greater predictive value than single factors is important. It is a pity that much research is not directed toward this goal. It is imperative that we put together all the factors that are known to relate to psi and thus provide optimum conditions for its manifestation. This is essential if our aim is to obtain less chaotic and more orderly results in ESP research.

## REFERENCES

Adcock, C. J., and Quartermain. (1959) 'Some problems in group testing of ESP.' *J. Parapsychol.*, **23**, 201–256

Astrom, J. (1965) 'GESP and the MPI measures' (Paper read at eighth annual convention of the Parapsychological Association, New York, 1965), *J. Parapsychol.*, **29**, 292–293. (Abstract)

Beloff, J., and Bate, D. (1970) 'Research report for the year 1968–69.' *J.S.P.R.*, **45**, 297–301

Bevan, J. M. (1947) 'The relation of attitude to success in ESP scoring.' *J. Parapsychol.*, **11**, 296–309

Bhadra, B. H. (1966) 'The relationship of test scores to belief in ESP.' *J. Parapsychol.*, **30**, 1–17

Carpenter, J. C. (1965) 'An exploratory test of ESP in relation to perceptual defensiveness.' J. B. Rhine *et al. Parapsychology: From Duke to FRNM*. Parapsychology Press, Durham, N. Carolina

Eilbert, L., and Schmeidler, G. R. (1950) 'A study of certain psychological factors in relation to ESP performance.' *J. Parapsychol.*, **14**, 53–74

Eysenck, H. J. (1967) 'Personality and extrasensory perception.' *J.S.P.R.*, **44**, 55–71

Freeman, J. A., and Nielsen, W. (1964) 'Precognition score deviations as related to anxiety levels.' *J. Parapsychol.*, **28**, 239–249

Green, C. E. (1966a) 'Extrasensory perception and the Maudsley Personality Inventory.' *J.S.P.R* , **43**, 285–286. (Abstract)

Green, C. E. (1966b) 'Extrasensory perception and the extroversion scale of the Maudsley Personality Inventory.' *J.S.P.R.*, **43**, 337. (Abstract)

Honorton, C. (1961) 'The relationship between ESP and manifest anxiety level.' *Proc. Parapsychol. Ass.*, No. 2

Humphrey, B. M. (1945) 'An exploratory correlation study of personality measures.' *J. Parapsychol.*, **9**, 116–123

Humphrey, B. M. (1950) 'ESP score level predicted by a combination of measures of personality.' *J. Parapsychol.*, **14**, 193–206.

Humphrey, B. M. (1951) 'Introversion–extraversion ratings in relation to scores in ESP tests.' *J. Parapsychol.*, **18**, 252–262

Johnson, M., and Kanthamani, B. K. (1967) 'The defense mechanism test as a predictor of ESP scoring direction.' *J. Parapsychol.*, **31**, 99–110

Kanthamani, B. K., and Rao, K. R. (1971) 'Personality characteristics of ESP subjects. I. Primary personality characteristics and ESP.' *J. Parapsychol.*, **35**, 189–207

Kanthamani, B. K., and Rao, K. R. (1972a) 'Personality characteristics of ESP subjects. II. The combined personality measure (CPM) and ESP.' *J. Parapsychol.*, **36**, 56–70

Kanthamani, B. K., and Rao, K. R. (1972b) 'Personality characteristics of ESP subjects. III. Extraversion and ESP.' *J. Parapsychol.*, **36**, 198–212

Kanthamani, B. K., and Rao, K. R. (1973) 'Personality characteristics of ESP subjects. IV. Neuroticism and ESP.' *J. Parapsychol.*, **37**, 37–51

Kahn, S. D. (1952) 'Studies in extrasensory perception: Experiments utilising an electronic scoring device.' *Proc. Amer. S.P.R.*, **25**, 1–48

Mangan, G. L. (1958) 'A review of published research on the relationship of some personality variables to ESP scoring level.' Parapsychological Monographs, No. 1, Parapsychol. Foundat., New York

McMahan, E. A. (1946) 'An experiment in pure telepathy.' *J. Parapsychol.*, **10**, 224–242

Nash, C. B. (1966) 'Relation between ESP scoring level and the Minnesota Multiphasic Personality Inventory.' *J. Amer. S.P.R.*, **60,** 56–62

Nash, C. B., and Nash, C. S. (1967) 'Relations between ESP scoring level and the personality traits of the Guilford-Zimmerman Temperament Survey.' *J. Amer. S.P.R.*, **61,** 64–71

Nicol, J. F., and Humphrey, B. M. (1953) 'The exploration of ESP and human personality.' *J. Amer. S.P.R.*, **47,** 133–178

Rao, K. Ramakrishna (1965) 'ESP and the manifest anxiety scale.' *J. Parapsychol.*, **29,** 12–18

Rao, K. Ramakrishna. (1966) *Experimental Parapsychology: A review and interpretation.* Charles C. Thomas, Springfield

Rivers, O. B. (1950) 'An exploratory study of the mental health and intelligence of ESP subjects.' *J. Parapsychol.*, **14,** 267–77

Schmeidler, G. R. (1950a) 'Some relations between picture-frustration ratings and ESP scores.' *J. Personality*, **18,** 331–344

Schmeidler, G. R. (1950b) 'ESP performance and the Rorschach test.' *J.S.P.R.*, **35,** 323–339

Schmeidler, G. R. (1952a) 'Rorschachs and ESP scores of patients suffering from cerebral concussion.' *J. Parapsychol.*, **16,** 80–89

Schmeidler, G. R. (1952b) 'Personal values and ESP scores.' *J. Abnorm. & Soc. Psychol.*, **47,** 757–762

Schmeidler, G. R. (1954) 'Picture frustration ratings and ESP scores for subjects who showed moderate annoyance at the ESP task.' *J. Parapsychol.*, **18,** 137–152

Schmeidler, G. R., and McConnell, R. A. (1958) *ESP and Personality Patterns.* Yale University Press, New Haven

Schmeidler, G. R. (1960) *ESP in relation to Rorschach test evaluation.* Parapsychological Monographs, No. 2, New York: Parapsychol. Foundat.

Shields, E. (1962) 'Comparison of children's guessing ability (ESP) with personality characteristics.' *J. Parapsych.*, **26,** 200–210

Smith, B. M., and Humphrey, B. M. (1946) 'Some personality characteristics related to ESP performance.' *J. Parapsychol.*, **10,** 169–189

Stuart, C. E., Humphrey, B. M., Smith, B. M., and McMahan, E. (1947) 'Personality measurements and ESP tests with cards and drawings.' *J. Parapsychol.*, **11,** 118–146

Van de Castle, R. L. (1958) 'An exploratory study of some personality correlates associated with PK performance.' *J. Amer. S.P.R.*, **52,** 134–150

# 4  Biological Aspects of PSI

**JOHN L. RANDALL**

## SYNOPSIS

*There is an evolutionary niche to correspond with almost every con-
ceivable mode of life on Earth and yet, so far as we know, there is no
species which depends critically on using extrasensory perception.
One is entitled to ask why, if psi is a reality, it has not been exploited
in the struggle for existence? There are, of course, a number of well
known phenomena in animal behaviour, of which bird navigation is,
perhaps, the most striking example, where the recognised sensory or
cognitive capacities of the animal appear to be strained to the limit
and perhaps beyond so that it becomes very tempting to invoke ESP.
But, otherwise, such evidence as we have on animal psi, and it is very
exiguous even as compared with that on human psi, suggests that psi
is just as exceptional in its occurrence and just as marginal in its
effects in the former as in the latter.*

*The author, a teacher of biology, discusses here various ways in which
psi might impinge on animal behaviour. The cases he deals with may
be divided into two categories (1) autonomous manifestations of psi
and (2) psi in human–animal communication. The former include
both spontaneous manifestations, as in the case of animal navigation,
and experimental phenomena such as precognitive awareness of
danger in a test situation or the ability to influence paranormally the
source of heat when the latter is governed by a random switching
mechanism. Examples of the second category are the performances
of pet animals who have been specially trained by their owners to
exhibit some psi ability or experiments where a human subject tries
paranormally to modify an animal's responses.*

*An unexpected development in 1968 has since elevated the field of
animal experimentation from being a topic of peripheral interest to
one in the forefront of current parapsychological research. This was
the publication in that year of certain findings by a distinguished
French biologist on the precognitive abilities of mice using entirely*

*automated testing equipment. His work was soon followed up in the United States and elsewhere and Table 4.1 shows the remarkable amount of corroboration which his claims have already received.*

*The application of automation to this area of research has not only introduced a new level of methodological sophistication but has succeeded in insulating the phenomenon from potential human psi effects to an extent that would have been impossible with a conventional setup. On the basis of this evidence the author feels he is justified in claiming that, if one fact has been established in the field of animal psi 'beyond all reasonable doubt' it is 'the existence of precognition in rodents'.*

*Finally, the author considers some recent work concerned with human PK influences on living tissues, either plant or animal, involving growth or regeneration. He goes on to discuss the implications of this for the problem of paranormal healing and points out that in any real life healing a number of interacting factors may be involved, physiological, psychological and even parapsychological. It is only by careful laboratory experiments that we can hope to disentangle these factors and ultimately discover what part if any psi plays in the therapeutic process.*

*Editor*

Experimental parapsychology began as an attempt to devise rigorous laboratory tests for certain human faculties, the existence of which had been strongly suggested by the study of spontaneous cases. In a similar manner 'animal parapsychology' arose out of observations which suggested the presence of extrasensory factors in the behaviour of certain animals. Such observations included apparent instances of telepathy between humans and animals, and certain cases of direction finding, or homing. In this chapter we shall be mainly concerned with the results of laboratory experiments designed to test hypotheses relating to the existence of psi in species other than man.

## ANIMAL NAVIGATION

The problems raised by the ability of wild animals to navigate over large distances were among the first to engage the attention of parapsychologists. In some cases of animal navigation it is fairly easy to suggest possible sensory mechanisms; in others the navigational powers of the animal seem to defy explanation in normal terms. In order to demonstrate conclusively that extrasensory faculties are involved it would be necessary to exclude completely all possible sensory factors, and this can seldom, if ever, be achieved. The matter is made more complex by the fact that in recent years a whole range of previously unknown sensory abilities has been demonstrated in certain species. Bats are now known to navigate by a kind of 'radar' utilising ultrasonic sound waves; bees and ants orientate themselves using polarised light from the sun; planarian worms, mud snails, fruit flies, and protozoa have been shown to respond to very weak magnetic fields (Brown, 1962); and it has recently been claimed that some monkeys can 'see' X-rays (*New Scientist,* **54,** 27th April 1972, p. 192). With such examples before him it is easy for the sceptic to claim that any instance of apparent ESP is due to some hitherto undiscovered sense. Indeed, many biologists regard the term 'extrasensory perception' as merely an admission of our ignorance, and argue that as biological knowledge expands so the number of cases of ESP will diminish. Fortunately for the parapsychologist, recent experimental work has made this view less tenable than it would have seemed ten years ago.

During the 1950s a determined attack on the problem of pigeon homing was made by Dr J. G. Pratt and his coworkers at the Duke University Parapsychology Laboratory (Pratt, 1964). The most plausible sensory hypothesis in this field is the sun-arc hypothesis put forward by Dr G. V. T. Matthews. According to this idea pigeons navigate by observing the movement of the sun through a small arc, which combined with a knowledge of the time of day enables them to determine the direction of home (Matthews, 1968). It is known that many, if not all, animals have built-in chronometers, or 'biological clocks', so that this part of the theory presents no difficulties. The chief drawback to the Matthews theory lies in the very short time that some pigeons need to observe the sun before they set off in the correct direction. Even when permitted to see the sun for only 10 seconds some birds appear to orientate themselves correctly, so that it must be assumed that they observe the arc traced by the sun during this very short interval, a feat which is clearly beyond any human eye. Pratt devised tests for a possible psi factor in pigeon homing, using movable lofts which could be placed in randomly chosen locations. Unfortunately the temperamental nature of the birds made it impossible to carry out a crucial test of the psi hypothesis, so that the question remains unresolved to this day. Pratt has suggested that pigeons might be trained to use lofts placed on board a ship, so that during a homing test the ship could be moved to a new position in the bird's absence.

This is an ingenious suggestion and it may be that some enterprising parapsychologist with a flair for working with pigeons will one day carry it out. Until this is done most biologists will no doubt prefer the sun-arc hypothesis, even though it involves attributing to the birds remarkably intricate powers of observation and calculation. It has recently been reported that some pigeons have found their way home even when their eyes were fitted with frosted contact lenses (*New Scientist,* **56,** 26th October 1972, p. 193). If this report is confirmed, it would appear to exclude all sensory hypotheses based on vision.

Similar to homing behaviour, but even more difficult to explain in sensory terms, are the cases of 'psi trailing'. These are cases where a dog or cat, left behind when a family moves home, subsequently finds its way to them over a considerable distance. Here the animal is not returning to a previously familiar environment (as in homing) but is somehow locating its master in totally unknown territory. Some of the best documented examples of psi trailing involve journeys of over a hundred miles, and there does not appear to be any way of accounting for them in terms of the known physical senses of the animal. The reader who is interested in such cases is referred to an excellent review by J. B. Rhine (Rhine, 1951).

## PSI COMMUNICATION BETWEEN MAN AND ANIMAL

Until quite recently most of the experimental work with animals has taken the form of a human 'agent' attempting to influence the behaviour of the animal without any direct sensory contact. One of the earliest experimenters in this field was the Russian neurophysiologist Vladimir Bechterev, who carried out some experiments with dogs before the First World War. Bechterev was a rival of the famous Pavlov, and at the time of the dog experiments he was Director of the Institute for the Investigation of the Brain in St Petersburg. The experiments consisted of silently willing the animals to carry out certain actions, and then observing their behaviour. Bechterev came to the conclusion that the dogs were responding to his unspoken thoughts, and he tried the effect of interposing screens of various materials between himself and the animals. After a fairly lengthy series of experiments in which attempts were made to exclude sensory cues, Bechterev concluded that some kind of thought transference had occurred between man and animal. His paper on the experiments appeared in the *Zeitschrift für Psychotherapie* (1924), but seems to have aroused little or no interest in the scientific world. An abbreviated form of it was subsequently published in the *Journal of Parapsychology* (1949).

Another isolated report of apparent animal ESP appeared in 1929 when the Rhines reported their investigations on a horse with alleged paranormal abilities. The horse, 'Lady', answered such questions as: 'What is the cube root of 64?', and 'How do you spell Mesopotamia?', by touching her nose on lettered and numbered blocks. The Rhines found that the horse only gave the correct answer when one or other of the humans knew it, which suggested that the animal was reacting to slight facial or bodily movements. A number of cases are on record in which animals are known to have reacted to movements so slight that they were barely noticeable to the humans present (for the most famous of these—the horse 'Clever Hans'—see Pfungst (1965)). In the case of Lady, however, this does not appear to have been the explanation, for even when steps were taken to exclude visual cues the successes continued, and the experimenters finally came to the conclusion that ESP was involved (Rhine and Rhine, 1929).

With the development of statistical methods in parapsychology several researchers tried to demonstrate psi effects between humans and animals using quantitative laboratory tests. Dr Karlis Osis tried putting cats into a T shaped maze and getting a human agent to will them to turn to the left or right, according to a randomised target order (Osis, 1952). The agent was enclosed in a cubicle with a one way window, so that he could not be seen by the cat. Under these conditions statistically significant results were obtained. Later the experiment was redesigned in order to test for clairvoyance, as distinct from telepathy, in the cat (Osis and Foster, 1953). In this version of the experiment the cats had to determine which of a pair of cups contained food, the target cup being unknown to both of the experimenters present. Electric fans were used to ensure that the air flow over the cups was always away from the direction of approach, so that the cats could not locate the target cup by smell. There was also a mild electric shock as 'punishment' for failure. Again, statistically significant results were obtained with some animals, suggesting the operation of some kind of psi effect.

One of the best animal psi experiments of the 1950s was that of Wood and Cadoret (1958) with a mongrel dog named 'Chris'. This dog had been taught to answer numerical questions by pawing at his master's sleeve the requisite number of times. The experimenters used the standard ESP cards, converting the five symbols into numbers according to a predetermined code. An extensive series of tests under increasingly stringent conditions eventually led to the situation where 'Chris' was guessing the cards correctly even when they were sealed in black envelopes and stacked in decks (the 'DT', or 'Down-Through' technique). One such series gave a positive critical ratio of 7·38, which would occur by chance less than once in a thousand million experiments. Since none of the humans present knew the order of the cards, direct telepathy between man and animal is ruled out. Either Chris was exhibiting 'animal clairvoyance' of a very high order, or one of the humans was acting as the ESP subject and transmitting the information to the animal by slight bodily movements.

Attempts to exert a psi influence on animals smaller than cats and dogs have been carried out by various workers, sometimes with a modest amount of success. In none of these cases, however, has there been adequate replication by other researchers. In view of the small number of biologically orientated parapsychologists this is not surprising, but it does mean that effects claimed by experimenters in this field must be viewed with caution. For those who are interested in pursuing this topic further we give references to work with protozoa (Richmond, 1952), woodlice (Randall, 1971), ants (Duval, 1971), moth larvae (Metta, 1971), and gerbils (Randall, 1972). Even if future research should confirm the existence of a psi effect in these situations it is by no means clear how such an effect is to be interpreted. The expression 'PK on living targets' commonly used by American writers implies that the organism is the passive recipient of a PK effect from the human agent, but there are a number of possible alternative interpretations. It would seem to be preferable to use some sort of neutral term, such as 'psi-interaction', to describe significant results in experiments of this type.

## ANIMAL PRECOGNITION

One way to ensure the exclusion of all known physical channels of communication in a psi experiment is to make it precognitive. The first worker to do this with animals was Dr Robert Morris of the American Psychical Research Foundation. He placed nineteen rats one by one in an open field maze, and measured the activity of each rat by counting the number of floor squares traversed by the rat during a two-minute time interval. Following this a second experimenter either killed the rat or spared it, according to whether an odd or even number had been assigned to the animal by a random number table in the second experimenter's possession. The expectation was that rats about to die would precognise the fact, and show less activity than those which would live (it is well known in animal psychology that rats undergoing stress show less activity than those which are not). Morris's experimental design is of considerable interest from several points of view; not only is it the first animal psi experiment to test for the existence of pre-cognition, but it also involves the use of somatic or emotional responses rather than presenting the animal with a fixed choice of two or more alternative actions. There is good evidence to suggest that some humans become subconsciously aware of impending disasters (including, in some cases, their own deaths), and react to them with various bodily symptoms (Barker, 1968). It is therefore of considerable interest to know whether such an effect can be demonstrated with rodents under laboratory conditions. In the event, sixteen of the nineteen rats used by Morris gave marginally significant results, but there have been no further replications reported.

In a second study using goldfish Morris measured the activity of the fish shortly before some of them were held aloft in a net—a condition which must be regarded as highly stressful for gold-fish. As before, the decision as to which fish were to be stressed was made by a random procedure after the activity measurements had been completed. The results showed that the goldfish which were about to be stressed displayed significantly greater activity than the others. This is in keeping with what is known about the behaviour of fish; whereas rats freeze when threatened, goldfish become more active in an effort to escape (Morris, 1970).

In view of the obvious interest of Morris's experiments, the reader is probably wondering why no other parapsychologists have attempted to replicate them. The answer probably lies in the fact that in the year following Morris's work a surprising new develop-ment occurred which has placed the existence of animal psi almost beyond question. The credit for initiating this new develop-ment goes to a distinguished French biologist who, in this in-stance, prefers to remain anonymous. In 1968, he and his young assistant published the results of the first entirely automated experiment in mouse precognition (Duval and Montredon 1968). The mouse was confined in a cage the floor of which was divided into two halves by a low barrier. A binary random number genera-tor delivered an electric shock through the floor of one half of the cage or the other, and a photocell device monitored the movement of the mouse each time it jumped the barrier. Recording was automatic, so that the experiment could be left running in the absence of the experimenter (*see* Figure 4.1). It was found that the mice were able to avoid going into that half of the cage which was about to receive the shock to an extent greater than chance expectation (odds against chance: about 1000 to 1). In analysing their results Duval and Montredon (pseudonyms) excluded from

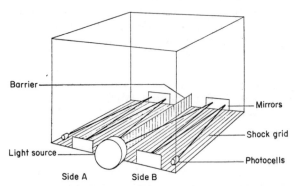

Figure 4.1    Diagram of testing cage. (Courtesy of *Journal of Parapsychology* **35**, 5, 1971.)

consideration all trials in which the mouse merely remained still (static behaviour) and all trials in which it jumped from one side to the other in response to a previously received shock (mechanical behaviour). Thus the analysis was confined to those trials where the animal moved from one side to the other for no apparent reason, an ingenious idea which enabled the researchers to separate the psi effect from the behavioural patterns caused by other factors. The decision to analyse in this way was, of course, made in advance.

Following the success of the French experiments, attempts were made to replicate them at the Institute for Parapsychology in North Carolina. Here Walter J. Levy and his co-workers carried out an extensive series of tests using random number generators of the type designed by Dr Helmut Schmidt (Levy, Mayo, André and McRae, 1971). At first the American workers obtained only marginally significant results, but as the researches continued it became clear that they too were obtaining strong evidence of the ability of mice to precognise electric shocks. Also, the more elaborate system of monitoring used by the Americans enabled them to record a greater number of trials and to look for further effects which could not be examined in the French work. Some of these secondary effects are of considerable interest when exploring the biological implications of this work. For example, Levy found that his animals showed significantly greater psi ability on trials which immediately followed a nonshock trial than on trials which were preceded by shock. The psi ability of the animal seemed to be inhibited for a short period after it had received the shock. He also found that animals which jumped around a lot between trials (when there were no shocks in either half of the cage) performed badly compared with those whose behaviour was less excitable (Levy et al., 1971, Levy and McRae, 1971, Levy, 1972). Both of these findings can be interpreted as suggesting that a stress-free state is conducive to psi. A further study showed that animals taken from cages which had been freshly cleaned and rearranged showed a marked improvement in scoring, with odds against the resulting difference being due to chance of about 50 000 to 1 (Levy and McRae, 1971). These results suggest that the animal's ESP ability is alerted whenever he is placed in an unfamiliar environment (such as a rearranged cage) but inhibited by states of stress. We may compare these conditions with the state of motivated but relaxed awareness which is considered by many workers to be the best attitude for success in human ESP experiments.

Table 4.1 summarises all experiments of this type known to have been performed at the time of writing. Most of these experiments involved mice, but in some of the American work jirds (gerbils) were used. It will be seen that all twelve experiments yielded positive results, a remarkable degree of consistency which is unfortunately rare in parapsychological research.

## ANIMAL PK?

The automated experiments in animal precognition provide the best evidence so far obtained for the existence of a psi faculty in species other than man. However, there have been other animal researches, and some of these have led to results that are exceedingly puzzling.

On a cold day in 1970 Dr Helmut Schmidt placed a cat in an unheated garden shed. The only warmth in the shed came from a 200 watt lamp which was coupled to one of the outputs of a binary random number generator. Whenever the generator produced a

+1 pulse the lamp was turned on and remained on until the generator produced a −1 pulse, whereupon it was turned off. According to probability theory the machine should have generated approximately equal numbers of +1 and −1 pulses, and the lamp should have been on about half of the time. In fact, Schmidt found that whenever the cat was in the shed the machine generated significantly more +1s than −1s, so that the animal received a longer period of warmth than expected. To ensure that the effect

Table 4.1   Precognition experiments with rodents

|  | No. of trials | No. of hits | % Hits | C.R. | p (two-tailed) |
|---|---|---|---|---|---|
| French work | 612 | 359 | 58·7 | 4·27 | $1·9 \times 10^{-5}$ |
|  | 376 | 208 | 55·3 | 2·06 | 0·04 |
|  | 8317 | 4415 | 53·2 | 5·67 | $1·3 \times 10^{-8}$ |
| American work | 1154 | 612 | 53·0 | 2·06 | 0·04 |
|  | 1308 | 704 | 53·7 | 2·77 | 0·006 |
|  | 1721 | 909 | 52·8 | 2·34 | 0·02 |
|  | 3547 | 1923 | 54·2 | 4·99 | $6·0 \times 10^{-7}$ |
|  | 1081 | 587 | 54·3 | 2·83 | 0·005 |
|  | 1533 | 829 | 54·1 | 3·19 | 0·001 |
|  | 2816 | 1538 | 54·6 | 4·91 | $9·1 \times 10^{-7}$ |
|  | 1186 | 627 | 52·8 | 1·97 | 0·05 |
|  | 640 | 373 | 58·3 | 4·19 | $2·8 \times 10^{-5}$ |

was not due to any nonrandomness inherent in the machine Schmidt ran control series in the absence of the cat, and also frequently reversed the two outputs of the generator. He found that the machine behaved perfectly normally when the cat was absent, but continued to turn on the lamp more frequently than expected when the cat was present. The odds against these results being due to chance were about 60 to 1.

Considering that perhaps the cat was exerting some kind of PK effect on the machine, Schmidt next tried an experiment in which cockroaches were subjected to electric shocks every time the machine generated a +1 pulse. Surprisingly, the cockroaches turned out to be negative scorers, since they received *more* shocks than they ought to have done according to chance. The two cockroach experiments completed by Schmidt gave odds against chance of 143 to 1 and 8000 to 1 respectively. As with the cat experiment, control series showed no abnormal behaviour on the part of the machine (Schmidt, 1970).

Since the Schmidt experiments, other workers have tried to see whether random number machines are affected by the presence of living organisms. Thus Graham Watkins tried the effect of putting 50 lizards of the species *Anolis sagrei* under a 250 watt heat lamp coupled to a random number generator, and found that the effect he obtained varied according to the weather conditions (Watkins, 1971). On hot, humid days the lamp stayed *off* more frequently than it should have done according to probability theory; whereas on cool, rainy days it came *on* more frequently. These results can be interpreted in terms of the biological needs of a cold blooded animal. Even more interesting are the results obtained by Levy and André during the summer of 1970, when they placed newly hatched chickens under a heat lamp connected to a Schmidt random number generator. It was found that under these conditions the lamp came on more frequently than expected on the chance hypothesis. As in all these experiments, the trial runs were interspersed with control runs for which the animals were removed, and the control runs showed only a random distribution of generated numbers (Levy and André, 1970).

Although chickens are vulnerable to cold and it is therefore to their advantage to have the lamp turned on, Levy and André reasoned that unhatched eggs would be even more vulnerable. The embryo within the egg relies entirely on the mother hen for warmth. The experimenters therefore tried the seemingly fantastic experiment of placing a box of live fertilised eggs under the heat lamp, replacing it with a box of dead eggs for the control runs. Again it was found that the runs with live eggs in the box showed a significant excess of +1s, while the controls gave no abnormal deviations (Levy, 1971).

If we are to take these experiments at their face value it appears as though living organisms are in some way able to influence the running of a random number machine. Some parapsychologists have suggested that the influence emanates from the experimenter rather than the organism under test, so that the effects described here are but another example of human PK. Since Schmidt has succeeded in demonstrating very convincingly the effect of human PK on machines of this type, such a suggestion appears very plausible. Against this hypothesis is the fact that many of these experiments were run with no experimenter anywhere near. In some cases runs were carried out overnight, with the experimenter at home and asleep some distance away. While this does not entirely rule out the possibility of a long distance PK effect from the experimenter, it does make this particular explanation rather less plausible than it would otherwise be.

## THE UTRECHT EXPERIMENTS

From the Parapsychological Division of the Psychology Laboratory at Utrecht University comes yet another approach to the study of animal psi (Schouten, 1972). This utilises positive rewards instead of electric shocks to provide incentive, and an experimental design which permits the operation of telepathy and clairvoyance rather than precognition. Mice are first given a period of training in which they are conditioned to press a lever in whichever half of the cage a light is turned on. Success in pressing the lever in the lighted half of the cage is rewarded by a drop of water; touching the wrong lever is punished by withholding the reward. The target side of the cage is alternated during training in such a way as to minimise the formation of any fixed habit patterns in the animal.

When training is complete, two mice are taken and placed in separate cages in rooms some distance apart. One mouse acts as the 'agent'; his cage contains two bulbs, mounted one in each half of the cage. The other mouse is the 'percipient', and his cage contains the two levers. The start of a trial is signalled by the sounding of a buzzer in the agent's cage, and a random selector then turns on one of the two lights in that cage. If the agent mouse can telepathically inform his colleague in the other room which of the two lights is on, then the percipient will be able to press the correct lever. The apparatus is so arranged that pressing of the correct lever by the percipient causes *both* mice to be rewarded with a water drop. All recording is automatic, so that the experimenter does not need to be present in either of the rooms during trials. The apparatus can also be used for testing under clairvoyant conditions, simply by removing the agent mouse and allowing the percipient to make his choices in the absence of any 'sendᴇ.'.

In his first report on experiments carried out with this equipment Sybo Schouten describes the results of testing 10 mice, each mouse completing six runs of 25 trials each. Three of the runs were done under 'telepathy' conditions (which in fact permitted the operation of either telepathy or clairvoyance) and three under clairvoyance conditions. The overall results were marginally significant, and there was a rather strong negative correlation between the scores of the mice on the telepathy runs and their scores on the clairvoyance runs ($r = -0.76$, $P = 0.01$). This latter finding indicates that those mice which scored well under telepathic conditions tended to do badly under clairvoyant conditions, and vice versa.

## EXPERIMENTS IN PARANORMAL HEALING

From the foregoing descriptions it can be seen that over the past forty years or so parapsychologists have developed a number of highly sophisticated and ingenious methods of testing for psi phenomena. It is therefore rather surprising to note that very seldom have these methods been applied to the field of paranormal healing, which is perhaps the one topic in parapsychology which offers any hope of being of direct value to mankind. Throughout recorded history there have been many reports of apparently inexplicable healings, generally (though not always) in a religious context. Of course, there have been many case studies of such phenomena, and some of these have been written up by medical authorities (West, 1957; Rose, 1971). However, until the work of Dr Bernard Grad and his colleagues, there does not appear to have been any attempt to carry out controlled laboratory tests of healing phenomena (Grad, Cadoret and Paul, 1961).

Grad was fortunate in having the services of a first class psychic healer, Oskar Estebany. Born in Hungary in 1897, Estebany entered the Hungarian army and served as a lieutenant during World War I. He is said to have first become aware of his healing abilities when as a cavalry officer he noticed that sick animals massaged by him recovered more quickly than they did under conventional treatments. Subsequently he went on to treat humans, and in spite of a general ban on psychic healing in that country, he won the support of several Hungarian physicians. Later he emigrated to Canada, where he submitted himself to a series of carefully controlled experiments under the direction of Dr Grad.

Grad's method was to inflict wounds on mice by removing a small area of skin under ether anaesthesia. The areas of the wounds were carefully measured by covering them with a piece of transparent plastic, tracing the outline with a grease pencil, and measuring the area on the plastic with a planimeter. Preliminary experiments covering a period of two years indicated that mice treated by Estebany healed more rapidly than those which were not. A full scale experiment was therefore set up, using a randomised block design to eliminate the possible effects of environmental variables. Care was taken to ensure that the experimenters who made the measurements did not know which mice were the treated ones. The wound healing in three groups of mice was compared: those treated by Estebany, those treated by persons not claiming any healing powers, and those given no treatment at all. Since it is well known that the fondling of mice tends to have a favourable effect on their physical condition, the healer was not allowed to handle the animals. The mice were in cages enclosed in heavy paper bags. One group of bags was sealed, and Estebany was only allowed to touch the outside of the bag; another group was left open at one end and the healer was allowed to put his hands inside the bag and touch the cage (but not the mouse). The treatments were given to the animals twice daily for periods of 15 minutes. After sixteen days there was a clearly significant difference between wounds on the mice treated by Estebany in open bags and those treated by other people, or not treated at all. The closed bag condition showed a difference in the same direction, but nothing like as clearly marked.

Subsequent experiments with Oskar Estebany have been no less remarkable. In two lengthy studies Grad found that barley plants watered with a 1% saline solution which had been held in the healer's hands grew better than plants watered with an untreated solution (Grad, 1963, 1964). The experimenter was able to show that the effect persisted even when the liquid was contained in sealed glass bottles, yet a detailed study by spectroscopic methods showed no detectable physical or chemical differences between the treated and untreated solutions. A further study of Estebany was made by Sister Justa Smith, head of the biology and chemistry departments at Rosary Hill College, Buffalo, in which she showed that the healer could apparently exert an accelerating effect upon the activity of the digestive enzyme trypsin (Smith, 1968).

Following the example of Grad, Graham and Anita Watkins have recently carried out an experiment in which human subjects tried to influence the recovery rate of mice which had been subjected to ether anaesthesia (Watkins and Watkins, 1971). Pairs of Swiss-Webster mice of the same sex and from the same litter were simultaneously rendered unconscious in identical etherisers. The human subject then concentrated on whichever of the two mice had been randomly chosen as the target. The aim was paranormally to induce the target mouse to awaken quickly, the other mouse being used as the control. Thirteen subjects were used in this experiment, of whom ten either claimed to have healing abilities, or had performed well in some other laboratory PK test.

The results were statistically highly significant overall, with odds against chance of about 100 000 to one. The three subjects who had no prior claim to be considered good psi subjects scored only at chance level, and so did one of the others. The nine remaining subjects, however, all scored above chance, four of them out-standingly so. The experiment has since been repeated by two different experimenters, using as subjects the four outstanding performers from the previous work (Wells and Klein, 1972). The results of this replication were significant, though not as pro-nounced as the results of the earlier experiment. The chief draw-back to this kind of research lies in the possibility of experimenter effects; even when the experiment is run with the experimenters 'blind', it is still conceivable that they might know, by ESP or in some other manner, which mouse is the target, and influence the outcome by their handling of the experiment. A completely automated design would seem to be the only answer to this problem.

A further series of researches which may be relevant to the problem of paranormal healing was carried out by Dr Jean Barry, a physician living in Bordeaux (Barry, 1966 and 1968). Human subjects were asked to concentrate on petri dish cultures of pathogenic fungi with the intention of retarding the growth of the organisms. Measurements showed a marked retardation of growth in the target dishes as compared with the controls. Finally, we may mention a pioneering study by Elguin in which a PK effect was apparently used to retard the growth of tumours in mice (Elguin, 1966).

If the effects reported by Grad and others are accepted one theory of paranormal healing can be definitely discounted, namely the view that it is entirely due to suggestion. Mice enclosed in paper bags are hardly likely to be susceptible to suggestion; barley seeds and pathogenic fungi even less so. This does not mean, of course, that suggestion plays no part at all in human healing; there is considerable evidence that it does. But there may also be an objective paranormal factor operating in some cases. Some of the healings at Lourdes, for example, are said to have occurred in spite of considerable scepticism on the part of the patient. It is likely that in the real life situations where healings occur we are dealing with a number of interacting factors, some physical, some psychological and some parapsychological. Only under controlled laboratory conditions can the various factors be separated for study, and it is for this reason that the kind of research initiated by Bernard Grad must be regarded as an extremely important contribution.

## CONCLUSIONS

At the close of a chapter such as this it would be satisfying to be able to draw all the threads together, giving an overall picture of the research and an indication of the direction in which it is leading. Unfortunately, this cannot be done. From among the heterogeneous collection of experiments described here there is only one fact which has, in the writer's opinion, been established beyond all reasonable doubt, namely the existence of precognition in rodents. The fully automated experiments with mice and gerbils have been replicated sufficiently often and yielded such clearly significant results that we are now justified in claiming this phenomenon as one of the most firmly established in parapsychology. To the workers in the field the establishment of one fact may not seem very much to justify the large amount of effort expended. To the academic biologist, however, even this one fact must appear revolutionary, since it seems to overthrow many of the present day assumptions of his science. It should not be forgotten that there have been several occasions in the history of science when the discovery of a single anomalous fact brought about the destruction of a well established theory and opened up entirely new avenues of thought. Whether this will happen with animal psi remains to be seen. Meanwhile the need is for further replication and extension of the researches already completed, so that the principles which underlie the phenomena can be clarified. Sufficient has already been achieved to make us certain that at least we are not wasting our time.

## REFERENCES

Barker, J. C. (1968) *Scared to Death*. Frederick Muller, London
Barry, J. (1966) 'Essais relatif à l'influence de la pensée sur la croissance des champignons.' *Revue métapsych.*, **2,** 43–66
Barry, J. (1968) 'General and comparative study of the psychokinetic effect on a fungus culture.' *J. Parapsychol.*, **32,** 237–243
Bechterev, W. (1949) ' "Direct influence" of a person upon the behaviour of animals.' *J. Parapsychol.*, **13,** 166–176
Brown, F. A. (1962) *Biological Clocks*. American Institute of Biological Sciences, Boston, Mass.
Duval, P. (1971) 'Exploratory experiments with ants.' *J. Parapsychol.*, **35,** 58 (Abstract)

Duval, P., and Montredon, E. (1968) 'ESP experiments with mice.' *J. Parapsychol.*, **32,** 153–166

Elguin, G. H. (1966) 'Psychokinesis in experimental tumorogenesis.' *J. Parapsychol.*, **30,** 220. (Abstract)

Grad, B., Cadoret, R. J., and Paul, G. I. (1961) 'The influence of an unorthodox method of treatment on wound healing in mice.' *Int. J. Parapsychol.*, **3,** 5–24

Grad, B. (1963) 'A telekinetic effect on plant growth.' *Int. J. Parapsychol.*, **5,** 117–133

Grad, B. (1964) 'A telekinetic effect on plant growth, II.' *Int. J. Parapsychol.*, **6,** 473–498

Levy, W. J. (1971) 'Possible PK by chicken embryos to obtain warmth.' *J. Parapsychol.*, **35,** 321 (Abstract)

Levy, W. J. (1972) 'The effect of the test situation on precognition in mice and jirds: a confirmation study.' *J. Parapsychol.*, **36,** 46–55

Levy, W. J., and André, E. (1970) 'Possible PK by young chickens to obtain warmth.' *J. Parapsychol.*, **34,** 303 (Abstract)

Levy, W. J., Mayo, L. A., André, E., and McRae, A. (1971) 'Repetition of the French precognition experiments with mice.' *J. Parapsychol.*, **35,** 1–17

Levy, W. J., and McRae, A. (1971) 'Precognition in mice and jirds.' *J. Parapsychol.*, **35,** 120–131

Matthews, G. V. T. (1968) *Bird Navigation. Second Edition,* Cambridge University Press, London

Metta, L. (1972) 'Psychokinesis on Lepidopterous Larvae' *J. Parapsychol.*, **36,** 213–221

Morris, R. L. (1970) 'Psi and animal behaviour: a survey.' *J. Amer. Soc. psych. Res.*, **64,** 242–260

Osis, K. (1952) 'A test of the occurrence of a psi effect between man and the cat.' *J. Parapsychol.*, **16,** 233–256

Osis, K., and Foster, E. B. (1953) 'A test of ESP in cats.' *J. Parapsychol.*, **17,** 168–186

Pfungst, (1965) '*Clever Hans*' New York: Holt, Rhinehart & Winston

Pratt, J. G. (1964) *Parapsychology: an Insider's View of ESP,* Doubleday, New York

Randall, J. L. (1971) 'Experiments to detect a psi effect with small animals.' *J. Soc. Psych. Res.*, **46,** 31–39

Randall, J. L. (1972) 'Two psi experiments with gerbils.' *J. Soc. Psych. Res.*, **46,** 22–30

Rhine, J. B. (1951) 'The present outlook on the question of psi in animals.' *J. Parapsychol.*, **15,** 230–251

Rhine, J. B., and Rhine, L. E. (1929) 'An investigation of a "mind-reading" horse.' *J. Abnorm. Soc. Psychol.*, **23,** 449–466

Rhine, J. B., and Rhine, L. E. (1929) 'Second report on "Lady", the "mind-reading" horse.' *J. Abnorm. Soc. Psychol.*, **24**, 287–292

Richmond, N. (1952) 'Two series of PK tests on paramecia.' *J. Soc. Psych. Res.*, **36**, 577–588

Rose, L. (1971) *Faith Healing.* Penguin Books, London

Schmidt, H. (1970) 'PK experiments with animals as subjects.' *J. Parapsychol.*, **34**, 255–261

Schouten, S. A. (1972) 'Psi in Mice: Positive Reinforcement.' *J. Parapsychol.*, **36**, 261–283

Smith, J. (1968) 'Paranormal effects on enzyme activity.' *J. Parapsychol.*, **32**, 281 (Abstract)

Watkins, G. (1971) 'PK in the lizard' (*Anolis sagrei*). *J. Parapsychol.*, **35**, 62 (Abstract)

Watkins, G., and Watkins, A. M. (1971) 'Possible PK influence on the resuscitation of anaesthetised mice.' *J. Parapsychol.*, **35**, 257–272

Wells, R., and Klein, J. (1972) 'A replication of a 'psychic healing' paradigm.' *J. Parapsychol.*, **36**, 144–149

West, D. J. (1957) *Eleven Lourdes Miracles.* Duckworth, London

# 5  In Search of the Consistent Scorer

J. G. PRATT

## SYNOPSIS

*Most parapsychologists, I imagine, would have to admit that there is nothing quite as rewarding as working with a special subject who can consistently produce significant scores. Unfortunately, it is a privilege granted to few, at any rate for more than a very brief period of time. A spate of such subjects appeared in the 1930s after the setting up of the Duke University Laboratory under J. B. Rhine and later, in England during the 1940s, S. G. Soal made his reputation on the basis of his work with two outstanding subjects. But, after that there was a lull and most of the important work done during the 1950s was not concerned with individual performances but with group results. Then, in the 1960s, a new star subject arose in Prague, of all unlikely places, in the person of a young man who is the hero of the present chapter. He was the discovery of a Czech parapsychologist and, as it turned out, was to surpass all previous guessing subjects known to the literature by dint of sheer staying power and productivity. For, although his scoring rate was never spectacular and his repertoire was confined to one particular binary guessing task, the doggedness with which he persevered at it coupled with his unfailing geniality, patience and modesty won him a unique and permanent place in parapsychological history.*

*The author, himself a veteran of the Duke Laboratory and today probably the world's most experienced investigator, became interested in this subject from almost the start of the latter's career and, since 1965, has been in charge of his investigation, commuting for the purpose whenever necessary between Charlottesville, Virginia and the Czech capital. But other visitors from abroad were never denied access to 'P.S.' and here the author gives special prominence to the visit of the three Dutch scientists in April 1963. He mentions that one of them, on returning to Amsterdam, wrote to him to say that they had gone to Prague sceptical of the claims being put out about this subject but 'had returned home convinced that they had witnessed the miracle of ESP'. As well they might, for, on the 2048 trials which* *they had run, P.S. had been correct on 1216 occasions and incorrect on only 832 occasions (where chance expectation is 50|50) giving odds of over $10^{14}$ to one against such a discrepancy being due to chance. Such evidence and that from subsequent experiments by the author himself where even more stringent precautions were taken against possible sensory cues leads the author to conclude that: 'the findings should be acceptable as convincing evidence of ESP for anyone who is intellectually prepared to weigh evidence bearing on the psi hypothesis and interpret it on its merits'.*

*The basic task throughout these investigations was that of identifying which side of a two colour card, the green or the white, was upper-most when the card was presented inside an opaque envelope. But a peculiar feature of this subject's performance which soon began to attract attention was that even when he was calling the wrong colour his calling was often highly consistent. That is, he would tend to give the same response whenever a specific card was presented even though, since it was concealed, he could never know, by any ordinary means, that it was that specific card. This odd phenomenon came to be known as the 'focusing effect' and increasingly became an object of interest in its own rights. For it began to appear that not only was there a focusing on specific cards but that often the calling was highly consistent whenever a specific envelope was presented regardless of what card it contained and that this persisted even when the envelope was concealed inside a larger envelope so as to exclude any normal means of identification. Indeed this tendency could have gone on indefinitely with the focusing shifting from the outer cover of one set of target packets to the jackets in which they, in turn, came to be inserted.*

*Here, for the first time, the author offers a plausible interpretation for this puzzling feature of his subject's guessing behaviour. He points out that P.S. began as a subject for Ryzl's research that was aimed at training clairvoyant ability under hypnosis. As such he was encouraged to regard his ESP ability like an X-ray that would be able to penetrate opaque materials. But, supposing that, for some reason, penetration failed to attain the target object, in this instance the coloured surface of the target card? Might he not fasten on some other layer of the target package? If so, this could well result in the identification of the envelope rather than its content and trigger off the kind of response that we are here calling a focusing effect.*

*So far, all the known guessing subjects eventually declined and ultimately lost their psi ability. P.S. appears to be no exception. At times, indeed, it has looked as if his usefulness as a subject was finally at an end and, at present, it seems uncertain whether it can last much longer. The author, however, having striven to keep P.S. from deteriorating for so long sees this as a challenge. Must psi ability inevitably decay, he wonders, or can we, with patience, prevent it? He suggests that we need persistent experimenters as much as we need consistent subjects.* Editor

Working with an individual who can give an outstanding psi demonstration has appealed to many investigators for a number of reasons. The rarity of persons who have had self-convincing psi experiences in everyday life predisposed the first investigators to think that persons who could demonstrate ESP under test conditions would also be rare. The high level of scoring such a subject usually maintains quickly gives a convincing demonstration of a real process at work, and an observer can more readily ascertain how the performance is affected by changes of conditions that he might impose. The evidence for some special process at work in a selected exceptional subject may be quite dramatic and can quickly become convincing even to an observer who is sceptical about psi. The advantages of working with a strong effect are self-evident insofar as the prospects of making more rapid advances in knowledge and understanding about the process are concerned.

At the same time, there are many questions that cannot easily be answered on the basis of individual results, since they raise issues that call for generalisations from the results of larger numbers of subjects. We must remind ourselves, therefore, that the appeal of working with special subjects offers no justification for neglecting problem centred research with unselected volunteers.

Viewing the developments in the field from the historical point of view brings to light striking trends and periodic changes in research strategy as regards the use of these two experimental approaches. The early decades were characterised by an out-standing number of experiments conducted with only one subject.* Even the exceptions to this rule mostly were studies carried out with only a small number of subjects. Yet there were exceptions which show, on closer examination, that investigators tried

* For details on this point it is convenient to refer to the comprehensive survey of the quantitative research on ESP during the six decades following the founding of the Society for Psychical Research in 1882 prepared by the research staff of the Duke Parapsychology Laboratory (Pratt, Rhine, Smith, Stuart, and Green-wood, 1940). Table 29 in that book gives a chronological listing of all of the ESP experiments carried out from 1882 until early 1939, and one column lists the number of subjects used in each study.

occasionally to find out if working with groups of unselected individuals would be productive in dealing with questions about ESP.

A dramatic shift in the numbers of subjects used in individual ESP experiments took place with the publication of the first results from the Duke laboratory (Rhine, 1934a). From that time onward the use of larger numbers of subjects in laboratory tests of ESP became the rule, though studies based upon the work of single individuals were still reported at a relatively lower level of frequency. On closer examination two of these exceptional instances prove to be cases in which investigators served as their own subjects (Pegram, 1937; Anonymous, 1938). In other cases investigators worked with individuals who came to them as possibly having special ESP abilities or who were outstanding among a larger number of persons tested (Rhine, 1934b, 1936; Warner, 1937; Riess, 1937; Martin and Stribic, 1938; Drake, 1938). Not to be overlooked is the fact that a relatively large proportion of the studies during this time from the European side of the Atlantic were one subject ESP tests, thus continuing the tradition that had earlier been strong there (Bender, 1936; Goldney and Soal, 1938).

In America the emphasis upon working with groups of volunteers became the rule almost without exception, whereas in Europe the emphasis continued to be placed upon finding individuals who were capable of demonstrating an outstanding ability and then working exclusively with them. There were, of course, exceptions to the rule on both sides of the ocean. The American way was strongly supported by J. B. Rhine; whereas the best example of the European preference was the work of S. G. Soal in England (Soal and Goldney, 1943; Soal and Bateman, 1954; Soal and Bowden, 1959). Indeed, the decades of the forties and the fifties were characterised by strong arguments within the field regarding which method was the proper one to use in psi research, with the Rhine position easily winning in terms of the number of adherents while the Soal approach gained stronger attention from the scientific community by virtue of the more impressive results obtained.

Another turning of the tide can now be seen as having taken place around the early sixties. Its beginning can be traced to the work of Milan Ryzl in Prague who emphasised the need for having outstanding subjects for research and who in 1961 started ESP tests with one subject, Pavel Stepanek (P.S.), who has now (1973) been working for more than a decade (*see* Figure 5.1). A score of scientists have to various degrees taken an active part in the investigations of his abilities in ways that the discussion of this case in depth in these pages and the references listed will amply illustrate.

Research history in parapsychology has also been made recently by other individuals claiming special psi abilities who have made themselves available as subjects in experiments suited to their talents. The names of Lalsingh Harribance, Ted Serios, and Nina

Figure 5.1   Pavel Stepanek during a break in testing at the University of Virginia, 1968.

Kulagina are already familiar in the literature as persons challenging our special attention, and others such as Ingo Swann and Bill Delmore are now on stage and ready to take their part as star subjects. Not all of these special persons have been studied to the point that they can all now be acclaimed for their scientific achievements, but there can be no doubt regarding the challenge that they make upon the research worker.

The current interest in research with outstanding subjects does not seem likely to become a full swing of the pendulum away from interest in experiments involving groups of unselected volunteers. Rather, there now appears to be widespread acceptance of the fact that work along both of these lines is needed. The current eagerness of the active research workers to see developments going forward in all areas of parapsychology is a welcome indication of scientific and professional maturity in the field.

The remainder of this chapter will focus attention upon the work with P.S. as one instance of research with an outstanding ESP subject. The reasons for choosing this subject are:

1.  A decade of sustained work makes him perhaps the outstanding test subject in the history of parapsychology in terms of the total number of trials performed as well as the period of time over which he has served successfully as an ESP subject in a reasonably continuous manner.
2.  The number of investigators who have worked with P.S. to the extent of satisfying themselves about the genuineness of his ESP abilities and reporting the results in the scientific literature is larger than for any other subject in quantitative tests.
3.  I have personally been directly involved in the work with P.S. during most of his career as a subject, and his case is the one that I know best from the recent period of renewed interest in special subjects.

A feature of the work of Ryzl (1962) that helped to capture the attention of other investigators was his claim that he had developed a special method of hypnotic training by which he could bring out the latent ESP capacities of normal persons who did not have any background of psi experiences. By the time he started working with P.S. in the summer of 1961 a number of investigators with whom he was in correspondence in other countries were quite prepared to take notice.

Late in 1961 the editors of the *Journal of Parapsychology* received a paper from Ryzl covering two experiments that he had carried out with P.S. with the assistance of his wife. Ryzl had not at that time fully overcome the language barrier, and there were understandably some questions that needed editorial clarification. Fortunately it became possible for me to visit Prague the following June, and as a result the first experimental report on work with P.S. was published shortly thereafter (Ryzl and Ryzlova, 1962).

When I arrived in Prague Ryzl suggested that we should also take advantage of the opportunity to carry out some joint research with P.S. The proposal was that I should designate the controls and decide upon a division of responsibilities between the two investigators that would make it possible for me to vouch for the ESP interpretation of the results.

I gladly accepted this opportunity and suggested that we could best serve the purpose in mind by working within the framework of the experimental procedure with which P.S. was already familiar. This provided a test for clairvoyance in which the subject attempted on each trial to say whether the white or the coloured side of a card hidden inside an opaque cardboard cover was presented facing him. The target cards were 75 mm wide and 125 mm long (approximately 3 × 5 inches) and the cardboard covers were wider and longer enough to insure that the cards would, when fully inserted, be completely shielded from view. Working under conditions that screened me from Ryzl and P.S., I randomised ten cards inside their covers then handed the set of concealed targets to Ryzl who held the covers one after the other in front of P.S. while he made his calls for the colours facing him. I observed the testing procedure and recorded the subject's responses, and after the run the two experimenters jointly recorded the order of the targets and checked the score.

This description obviously only provides a general idea of the experimental method. Full details regarding the materials used in the experiments done over the decade and the test procedures followed would be too tedious and lengthy to repeat here. Anyone wishing to study them should refer to experimental reports prepared by the investigators who, usually working in teams, participated at various times in this research, many of which are included in the references listed at the end of this chapter. A lengthy survey and reappraisal of the decade of research has been presented (Pratt, 1973). This chapter will of necessity be limited to giving some of the highlights of the results.

On the question regarding whether the success of the research was made possible through a hypnotic method for training ESP there is simply no basis for a conclusion. Ryzl did not carry out any controlled tests to separate the factor of hypnosis from other conceivable ones, such as the experimenter's belief and enthusiasm which could have aroused favourable expectations in his subjects. Three other investigators have attempted to test his hypothesis on training ESP without obtaining any clear support for it (Beloff and Mandleberg, 1966; Stephenson, 1965; Haddox, 1966).

An aspect of the results with P.S. that is of special scientific interest is his ability to show successful ESP scoring on numerous occasions in the presence of many different investigators. Research progress in parapsychology has been retarded by the fact that many outstanding ESP subjects who performed well in the presence of experimenters to whom they were accustomed would drop to a chance level of scoring when other observers were introduced into the test situation. P.S. has been a striking exception to this rule. The first indication of his reliability in the presence of a stranger was given in the first published report, since P.S. had not met Ryzl's wife until she was introduced to him at the start of that particular experiment. The work done during my first visit showed that even the presence of a scientist from abroad did not stop his success (Ryzl and Pratt, 1962). The probability level of significance reached in that work was only 0·001, which was modest in comparison with the level of $10^{-9}$ reached in the experiment done with the same testing procedure by Ryzl and Ryzlova (1962, Experiment I).

On my second visit to Prague (January 1963) two experiments were carried through. The first one (2000 trials) used the basic design described above: coloured cards concealed in opaque cardboard covers (Ryzl and Pratt, 1963a). The results, at a higher level of scoring than we had obtained previously, were comparable to the scoring rate achieved in the work with Ryzl and his wife as coexperimenters.

The second experiment (5000 trials) involved a basic change in procedure. Before the experiment twenty white/green cards were sealed in twenty cardboard envelopes. These preparations were made in a way that insured that neither experimenter could have any knowledge of the position of any card inside its envelope. The twenty envelopes were then identified by marking them with a number and letter code on each side. After that the sealed envelopes were randomised and concealed inside individual cardboard covers by one experimenter working alone in a room with the doors closed, then both experimenters observed the testing procedure during the run and the recording and checking of the results. This procedure was repeated over a period of five days until the 250 runs were completed (Ryzl and Pratt, 1963b).

The results on the concealed targets were highly significant, particularly so because of a surprising aspect of the subject's performance. This was the fact that P.S. did not show the same general level of ESP performance for all of the concealed targets. Rather, he exhibited strong calling preferences on about half of them while he gave only chance responses in relation to the others.

We named this tendency of the subject to favour particular targets the 'focusing effect'. It has been the outstanding feature of his test performance throughout the decade and the one that has received the most attention from investigators. We will return to this topic shortly.

Before doing so, however, we should finish tracing the evidence bearing upon the stability of ESP performance P.S. showed with different experimenters and under different circumstances. Also, it will be worthwhile to consider the strength of the evidence for ESP that his performance provides, since some readers will doubtless still be interested in the question whether ESP really occurs.

A further stage of demonstrating this subject's scoring reliability in the presence of strangers was reached in April 1963 when three Dutch scientists went to Prague. They expected to spend two days there talking with Ryzl about his hypnotic training method, but they readily agreed to a shift in plans when Ryzl invited them to conduct their own experiment with P.S. Ryzl introduced them to the subject, provided testing materials, made available the two rooms in his home that he used for the research, and then largely stayed out of the situation. He only came in occasionally to encourage P.S. and to find out how things were going.

Their experiment (Ryzl, Barendregt, Barkema, and Kappers, 1965) used cards hidden in envelopes and left unchanged throughout the investigation. The envelopes were randomised before each run with respect to the sides upward inside cardboard covers. One of the investigators wrote me after returning to Amsterdam and said that they had gone to Prague sceptical about the claims Ryzl had been making but had returned home convinced that they had witnessed the miracle of ESP. The results of their test reached a level of significance with a probability of chance occurrence of less than $10^{-14}$. In 2048 trials P.S. had called the colour correctly 1216 times and had missed it 832 times (*see* Table 5.1).

The next stage of separation of P.S. from familiar test situations in which he had previously succeeded was reached in November 1963. Visiting experimenters 'borrowed' the subject from Ryzl and found a new location for their experiments (one with which P.S., however, was personally familiar). The investigators used their own test materials that they had brought in their luggage. Significant results were obtained in three experiments carried out under these circumstances (Pratt, 1964; Pratt and Blom, 1964; Blom and Pratt, 1968).

**TABLE 5.1**  Details of responses to the sixteen target sets of the experiment in Prague by visiting Dutch scientists (*see* Ryzl, Barendregt, Barkema and Kappers, 1965)

| Sets without significant results on concealed objects | | | | Sets with significant results on concealed objects | | | |
|---|---|---|---|---|---|---|---|
| Concealed | | Calls | | Concealed | | Calls | |
| Envelope | Card | W | G | Envelope | Card | W | G |
| C | W | 37 | 22 | A | G | 4 | 69 |
| D | G | 35 | 34 | B | W | 33 | 22 |
| (Total calls) | | (72 | 56)* | | | (37 | 91) |
| M | W | 9 | 68 | E | G | 11 | 56 |
| N | G | 3 | 48 | F | W | 37 | 24 |
| | | (12 | 116) | | | (48 | 80) |
| R | G | 4 | 59 | G | G | 21 | 38 |
| S | W | 13 | 52 | H | W | 39 | 30 |
| | | (17 | 111) | | | (60 | 68) |
| 3 | G | 17 | 54 | K | W | 29 | 36 |
| 4 | W | 8 | 49 | L | G | 17 | 46 |
| | | (25 | 103) | | | (46 | 82) |
| 9 | W | 17 | 38 | T | W | 29 | 32 |
| 10 | G | 18 | 55 | U | G | 17 | 50 |
| | | (35 | 93) | | | (46 | 82) |
| 13 | G | 9 | 53 | 1 | W | 36 | 26 |
| 14 | W | 13 | 53 | 2 | G | 4 | 62 |
| | | (22 | 106) | | | (40 | 88) |
| 15 | G | 22 | 48 | 5 | G | 14 | 61 |
| 16 | W | 13 | 45 | 6 | W | 25 | 28 |
| | | (35 | 93) | | | (39 | 89) |
| (Totals—7 sets) | | (218 | 678)‡ | 7 | W | 10 | 56† |
| | | | | 8 | G | 27 | 35 |
| | | | | | | (37 | 91) |
| | | | | 11 | W | 57 | 18 |
| | | | | 12 | G | 10 | 43 |
| | | | | | | (67 | 61) |
| | | | | (Totals—9 sets) | | (420 | 732)‡ |

General comment: Each card remained hidden and undisturbed in its envelope throughout the experiment, the envelope being randomly inverted or left the same in its cover before each run. The covers were always presented with the same side uppermost.
(See footnotes to Table 5.1 on p. 105)

Finally, P.S. visited the University of Virginia for further ESP testing on three occasions. The first visit in 1967 was highly productive (Pratt and Roll, 1968; Roll and Pratt, 1968), and the second one in 1968 was even more so (Keil and Pratt, 1969; Pratt and Keil, 1969; Pratt, Keil and Stevenson, 1970; Pratt, Stevenson, Roll, Blom, Meinsma, Keil and Jacobson, 1968).

At the time of the third visit in early 1969 P.S. was in a relatively unproductive stage and the results were not significant. Since that last visit to Charlottesville the work has been continued through several more visits to Prague with relatively little new evidence of ESP, but there have been occasional periods with noteworthy success (Pratt and Ransom, 1972; Pratt and Keil, 1972).

When asking whether this research has provided results for which ESP is the only reasonable interpretation, we should first consider the best evidence available. If the best-controlled experiments provided strong evidence supporting the ESP hypothesis, we can reasonably assume that P.S. was also using ESP in other tests that were controlled less rigorously but for which no actual weakness in the experimental conditions has ever been demonstrated.

An experiment which provided especially strong evidence for ESP was one of those carried out in Prague in November 1963 (Blom and Pratt, 1968). This study grew out of the earlier work by the Dutch group. They had realised after further reflection that their results supported the ESP hypothesis but that the procedure they had used did not provide conclusive evidence of ESP responses to the concealed colours. In their test the coloured cards remained inside the envelopes in the positions in which they were placed originally. Whenever the envelopes were turned over inside the

---

* First day: 21W, 43G; second day: 51W, 13G.
Thus it is clear that set C/D elicited a strong 'white' response on the second day, which is sufficient to show that the strong 'green' tendency shown on the other six sets with insignificant results on the concealed objects cannot be attributed solely to a general tendency to over-call green.

† Set 7/8 shows a significant relation between the side of the concealed target uppermost and the colour called ($P < 0.002$), but the response preferences are opposite to the colours presented. This is sufficient to suggest that the ESP responses on the individual trials were made to the envelope sides and that they had been incorrectly associated by P.S. with the placement of the card concealed inside.

‡ A chi-square test of the difference between the 'white' and 'green' response tendency in the two groups of sets is highly significant ($P < 10^{-7}$), which shows that the strong tendency to call 'green' on the sets with insignificant results on the concealed targets was held in check to some degree by the responses to the concealed targets in the other nine sets.

covers in the process of randomising the material, the cards thus followed along invariably. It was not possible, therefore, to be sure that the subject's responses were linked only with the cards concealed under two layers of opaque cardboard. At least some of the responses could have occurred in relation to the envelopes which were hidden only by the single layer of the cardboard covers.

In either case the results provided evidence of ESP since everyone having firsthand experience with the situation agreed that there was no way that P.S. could have known on a sensory basis which way the envelopes were facing. Nevertheless it was clear that the evidence for ESP would be objectively strengthened for others if it could be clearly shown that the subject could indeed respond to the doubly-enclosed card. Furthermore it would be of some theoretical interest to know that ESP is capable of detecting colour in the complete darkness surrounding the doubly-enclosed cards.

We planned an experiment specifically to deal with these questions. This involved a daily session of 1000 trials and covered four days. The test materials were forty sealed cardboard envelopes, each one containing a white/green card and two sets of eight cardboard covers in which the envelopes were concealed when they were presented to the subject. The cards were put in the envelopes by a double-blind procedure to insure that neither experimenter could know their positions. This was part of the experimental procedure which was carried out four separate times during the experiment, before each daily session.

During the testing procedure itself these envelopes were randomised by one experimenter working alone in a closed room and were concealed, eight at a time, inside the cardboard covers (*see* Figure 5.2). The two sets of covers were used alternately. The second experimenter was testing P.S. with one while the other set was being prepared.

Both experimenters participated in recording the targets (the sides of the concealed envelopes presented upward) at the end of each run and in tabulating the results at the end of each daily session. Duplicate copies were made of all of the data, and one of these was kept by each experimenter.

The random shifting of the cards among the envelopes before each of the four sessions made it possible to separate the effect of the cards from that of the envelopes. This degree of independence justified applying separate statistical treatment to the two sets of data. The results for the cards showed that P.S. had scored a highly significant number of hits on colour ($P < 2 \times 10^{-6}$). Overall, there was also some consistency of response upon the forty envelopes, but this was at a much lower level of significance than that found for the forty cards. The 'envelope effect' thus can

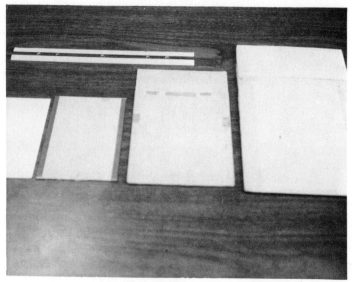

Figure 5.2   Close-up of materials used in many of the ESP tests. Left to right: card, white side up; cardboard envelope; cardboard cover; jacket used for concealing cover (with envelope and card enclosed) in investigations of the focusing effect.

reasonably be interpreted as an artifact of the strong responses to colour and a result of the partial randomisation of the cards in the envelopes (daily instead of before each trial).

Subsequent to the publication of the formal report on this research one of the experimenters reported an evaluation of the results on colour in terms of a 'majority vote' analysis applied to the forty targets for each day. In this analysis all of the responses made each day for each of the envelopes were scored as a 'hit' if a majority of them agreed with the position of the card sealed inside and as a 'miss' if the majority was wrong for the placing of the card. Over the four days the majority call was correct for 96 cards and incorrect for 56 (the remaining 8 cards having received tie votes or an equal number of white and green responses). A difference as large as 40 in a random sampling of 152 observations where the expectation is a zero difference has a probability of occurring by chance less than 2 times in 1000 cases. Even this conservative basis of evaluation thus provides adequately significant evidence supporting the conclusion that P.S. was responding to the colours.

In designing and carrying out the experiment we carefully considered and controlled against the possibility that any physical characteristic of the card, such as warpage, could have provided any kind of sensory cue through the two covering layers of cardboard. The testing conditions also ruled out other conceivable possibilities of experimenter error and misinterpretation except that of a deliberate hoax perpetrated by both experimenters. This is a level of safeguarding beyond that ordinarily required in scientific work, and the findings therefore stand as unambiguous evidence for ESP.

The other research that I would point to as offering the strongest evidence for ESP belongs to a later stage of the research, the period of the second visit to the University of Virginia in February–March 1968. These results are covered in a research report which emphasised the fact that a third experimenter joined the regular team of two investigators for the purpose of actively scrutinising the procedure and evaluating the adequacy of the experimental safeguards (Pratt, Keil, and Stevenson, 1970). Before this work was done a change had occurred in the test performance of P.S. in that the focusing effect had become strongly and unmistakably linked with one or another aspect of the covering materials used to shield the inner target card rather than with the colours themselves. In fact, for a time P.S. primarily showed strongly patterned responses on the exposed outer cardboard covers. There were rarely any significant results found on the hidden cards during that period. Then it was discovered that the strong response habits formed on the exposed surfaces of the containers continued without any disruption when those objects were made the ESP targets by concealing them in larger containers (Stanford and Pratt, 1968).

The two significant experiments in which Stevenson served as a third observer yielded highly significant patterned responses on concealed objects when specific controls were used to rule out recognition of them on any conceivable sensory basis (sight, weight, shape, sound, or the unconscious transfer of cues from one or both of the experimenters). The experimental procedure is illustrated in Figure 5.3a–f.

Articles on these and related investigations appeared in *Nature*

(Pratt *et al.*, 1968) and *New Scientist* (Beloff, 1968) and there was extensive discussion afterward in the letter columns of both periodicals. One critic commented that every possible avenue of sensory leakage had been eliminated except that of smell. This possibility can be dismissed as not being applicable for two reasons:

1. The whole stack of objects were all at approximately the same distance (about 18 inches) from the subject's nose during the run, and the specific sources of odours cannot be pinpointed under those circumstances.
2. Nevertheless in a later series the step was taken of wrapping some of the concealed objects in odour shielding plastic, and the same patterning of significant responses to those objects continued as had been observed previously (Pratt and Ransom, 1972).

In view of the very high levels of significance reached in these experiments, the findings should be acceptable as convincing evidence for ESP for anyone who is intellectually prepared to weigh evidence bearing upon the psi hypothesis and interpret it on its merits.

We can return now to the consideration of the focusing effect, examining whether it really began early in the research as a focusing upon particular *cards* but shifted to a focusing upon the *shielding containers* later on, and characterising the efforts made to explain it in parapsychological or familiar psychological terms.

Having struggled with this problem for longer than I like to admit, I finally see what I think is the light of better understanding at the end of the tunnel of puzzlement. My thinking on this topic has been presented fully in a longer survey of the research with P.S. that has recently been published (Pratt, 1973). Here I will try to give the gist of the matter more briefly.

In a nutshell, I now think that the evidence from the whole decade of research shows that P.S. has been using throughout basically the same approach to the assigned task, and what the experimenters took to be a strong shift in his performance about midway through the decade was due to a mistaken interpretation forced upon the findings during the earlier period of the research. The mistake was caused by the unwarranted assumption that the primary point of contact P.S. was making with the target material was the one the investigators intended, the concealed coloured card. After all, the experiments were designed from the inside out,

(a)

(b)

Figure 5.3
Steps in testing procedure
used at the University of
Virginia in 1968. (a) First
experimenter in random-
ising cubicle. (b) Assemb-
ling targets by random
numbers. (c) Passing pre-
pared targets to second
experimenter. (d) Second
experimenter   receiving
targets through 'neither-
way vision' opening in
screen. (e) Cutting stack
of targets by a random
digit. (f) The subject calls
concealed targets as he
lays each packet aside
and both experimenters
record.

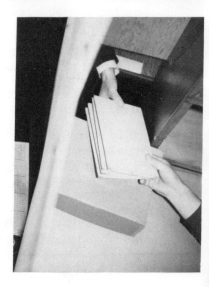

(c)

(d)

(e)

(f)

and only the central object, the white/green card, was supposed to play a role in eliciting the subject's ESP response. The subject always knew that the card was hidden within all its wrapping and he was told to respond to the colour facing him. His results as evaluated in terms of the way the cards were facing were significant, and he always responded as requested in that he responded with a choice between the two colours on every trial, even when he was wrong. What could seem more logical, therefore, than that the experimenters should conclude that P.S. was regularly trying to call the cards while ignoring other aspects?

I submit that a close examination of the data shows that this is a false view of what P.S. was doing even from the beginning. Rather, he responded to the test packet presented to him on each trial from his own point of view as an observer, trying to 'see' from the outside inward in the effort to reach the target colour.

From what Ryzl (1962, 1966) has said about his method of using hypnosis to prepare his subjects to demonstrate ESP it is clear that he emphasised a close connection between ESP and normal vision. Subjects were urged during hypnosis to develop strong visual imagery; they were told that they would be able to 'see' an object with their eyes closed, then when it was placed behind them.

Just suppose that his approach had somewhat the same effect as telling a subject in hypnosis that he had X-ray vision and could see the card right through the shielding material. Suppose further that a subject working with such a mental set was not always capable of penetrating to the centre of the target packet. What could we logically expect the data to show under such circumstances?

Several kinds of response effects might occur:

1. One is really an absence of any definable effect, since there might be some packets for which P.S. would not form any association, either sensory or extrasensory, and for them he would only give random or chance calls.
2. Another kind of effect might be significant response preferences of a sensory nature based upon visual associations linked with the exposed surfaces of some of the packets.
3. A third kind of effect, the first one depending upon ESP, would be nonrandom responses to the first concealed layer of the packet. In most of the earlier experiments this would have brought him into contact with the envelopes, while in

others he would have reached the cards (when no envelopes were used). In the former case, it seems obvious that the rule of parsimony of hypotheses would say that we should attribute the effect to the envelopes rather than the cards they contained to the extent this can account for the results.

This opinion gains strong support from the data. Efforts that were made in the original reports to explain the results as ESP responses to the cards required the interpretation that ESP hitting and ESP missing were occurring in every conceivable combination on the faces of the different cards (Ryzl and Pratt, 1963b). Taken from the point of view of responses to the envelopes, the same results do not represent hitting and missing tendencies but only regularities of response based upon associations formed on an ESP basis between the surfaces of the envelopes and the two 'colour' responses.

Unfortunately it is not possible to check in the data of all of the early experiments for all of the kinds of responses outlined above. In many series no record was made of the side of the outer cover that was presented upward on each trial. However, we can infer some things about responses to the covers because of the fact that the concealed targets were not shifted about among the covers within the test series.

There is, fortunately, one experiment in which we can say in detail how the subject's responses were related to the covers. This is the research by the Dutch team. In that study the covers were always presented with the same side upward, whereas in other experiments both sides were used randomly. For the present purpose, therefore, we will limit ourselves to a brief statement of the findings from a detailed re-examination of the Dutch experiment (Ryzl, Barendregt, Barkema and Kappers, 1965).

In that experiment sixteen target packets, designated 'sets' in the report, were used. Each one consisted of the outer cardboard cover, the inner cardboard envelope, and the innermost white/green card (which remain undisturbed in its envelope throughout the experiment). The target sets were identified by code markings on the two sides of the envelopes, letters being used for one group of eight sets and numbers for the other. The question raised here is: What does a close examination of the data for each target set reveal regarding how P.S. was responding to it?

1. No sets were found among the sixteen to which merely random responses were made.
2. For seven sets the data reveal a significant tendency to respond only to the cover by calling it either 'white' or 'green' without regard to the position of the target concealed inside. These seven sets are: C/D, M/N, R/S, 3/4, 9/10, 13/14, 15/16 (*see* Table 5.1). For all except the first of these P.S. showed a strong preference for calling green; and for C/D he showed a shift in preference between the two days of the experiment, white calls being strongly predominant on the second day.
3. The other nine sets (A/B, E/F, G/H, K/L, T/U, 1/2, 5/6, 7/8, 11/12) yielded results indicating that P.S. responded significantly to the concealed targets as based upon a difference in his calls on each set in relation to which side of the concealed envelope was upward. These are the only sets in the experiment that gave results relevant to the occurrence of ESP. Eight of these sets were called in a manner consistent with the positioning of the cards inside the envelope, but one (7/8) was called in a manner that disagreed with the placing of the card. It is interesting to see that the 'missing tendency' on this card was due entirely to those trials when side 7 of the envelope was presented upward. On those trials the white side of the card was facing P.S., but he called white only 10 times and green 56 times. When the other side was upward he named the colour correctly more often than not (35 green to 27 white), but this difference is not significant.

There is no reason why we should not suppose the results on these nine concealed targets were primarily ESP responses to the envelopes comparable to the sensory association of 'white' or 'green' to the covers of the other seven sets. One might assume, of course, that ESP responses were being made only to the cards while the envelopes were ignored. However, this would be a gratuitous and unparsimonious assumption to make. Furthermore, choosing the ESP-of-colours hypothesis raises the embarrassing question of why the white card facing toward envelope side 7 should have been the only target to evoke strong psi missing among the eighteen faces of these nine cards.

Where does this re-examination of the data of the Dutch series leave matters as regards the evidence for ESP? Just where it was, since the outer covers were used to rule out sensory cues from the enclosed envelopes and the experimenters were satisfied that they were adequate for this purpose. It only puts in doubt the interpretation given in the published report that the data provided highly significant evidence of ESP responses to the cards.

Some evidence of an ESP effect on the cards from this experiment that is statistically valid is the fact that eight out of nine cards were correctly indicated by the majority vote principle. Because of the small number of targets this result is scarcely sufficient to allow us to say that this experiment alone established ESP identification of the cards. But this is why Blom and I carried out the experiment later that same year to deal explicitly with this question. That work, as already stated, did provide clear evidence that P.S. was responding to the colours by ESP.

The investigators became aware only about the middle of the decade that the response tendencies on aspects of the covering materials were stronger than the ESP responses to the cards. Looking back now with the advantage of hindsight and in the light of such additional new considerations as are offered here, we can see that this was probably not a basic change in the mode of response. Close re-examination of other earlier experiments reveals that some of the highly significant response effects that occurred were mistakenly linked with the concealed cards at the time. They should have been recognised as ESP responses associated instead with the concealed envelopes in some instances, and they could have been responses to the exposed covers for other target objects. Detailed discussion of these and other features of the data that call for reappraisal is given elsewhere (Pratt, 1973).

It does seem, however, that a gradual change in the test performance of P.S. was taking place through the years. He showed a gradual weakening of his ESP responses to the cards, while his patterned responses to aspects of the covering materials were becoming relatively stronger. In fact, the research of the last three years has mostly produced evidence of strong focusing effects on the exposed surfaces of the outside containers, and we may be approaching the time when we will have to admit that the subject's unconscious ESP process has finally become fully inhibited in the test situation by sensory responses, which also seem to be unconscious in this instance.

Two distinct hypotheses have been offered as possibly accounting for the focusing effect. Ryzl (1968) thinks the explanation may require recognising some sort of new energetic effect that is parapsychological in nature. He says this energy somehow becomes impregnated into an object when the subject makes contact with it by ESP and these impregnations accumulate and form a 'trace' in the object which tends to evoke the same ESP response in the subject when that object is presented on a later trial. Other investigators (Pratt and Keil, 1969; Keil, 1971; Pratt and Keil, 1972) have suggested an explanation following familiar psychological principles of learning. Ryzl has not been able to find any way of analysing the data now available to give crucial support to his hypothesis, while the converging lines of evidence as touched upon here seem to be lending support to the explanation along familiar psychological lines.

The typical consistent ESP test scorer as discussed in this chapter is a person who will be successful as a subject for only a limited span of time. All such selected persons in the annals of the research have sooner or later ceased to give good scores, and as a rule work with them was discontinued on the ground that they had lost their ESP ability. This is an explanation that explains nothing. I have long insisted that the decline of test performance to the chance level in a person who has demonstrated his ability to show consistently successful ESP scoring should not be a sign to end the research but a challenge to new research directed toward finding out why the level of success has dropped and with the aim of bringing the performance once more to its maximum strength.

The direction of parapsychological research which I would recommend to my colleagues, both present and future, is thus one that is really new and unexplored. This is the direction of being persistent experimenters in the search for really consistently successful psi test scorers. Successful research in this new direction would do much to consolidate past gains in parapsychology and to insure sound and accelerating progress in the field for the years ahead.

My colleague Ian Stevenson, an occasional participant in the research with P.S. and always an enthusiastic supporter of the investigations, commented that the subject comes across in the published reports as a kind of guessing machine. Since my knowledge of the case showed the degree to which this impression was justified, I looked for the reason for it. Most of the reports covered investigations carried out by visiting experimenters over brief periods of time that left little opportunity to go deeply into personal and personality aspects of the research. It is not surprising, therefore, that the emphasis was put on objective features of the work. The testing procedure was ready-made, and it was presented to the visitors as the only method they could use with P.S. if they expected to observe successful ESP performance.

For many of these visiting investigators the important thing was testing the claim that P.S. was so stable in demonstrating his psi ability that he could produce significant results within a short time. The emphasis in most of the series was therefore upon experimental safeguards; and in the ensuing reports, upon the highly significant results that had been obtained. This manner of doing the work and reporting it is understandable, but to recognise this fact is not to say that it is excusable. Behind the initials 'P.S.' there is a real person who must be considered by the investigators in the efforts to evaluate the work with this selected subject. It is not possible to present here in detail the personal aspects of the research, but the reader is at least entitled to feel that he knows who Pavel Stepanek is. Another source giving more detailed information is available for those who desire to go further into the psychological issue (Pratt, 1973).

P.S. was thirty years of age when he began working with Ryzl in 1961. He was the only son of working parents in a family of very modest economic circumstances (his father worked as a street sweeper). Since the first seven years of his life P.S. has lived through the series of historical crises and changes that have swept over Czechoslovakia. These developments have taken a heavier toll from him than from the average Czech citizen because of the fact that he is by nature a very retiring and cautious person. Indeed, he carries a heavy load of anxieties about many situations that he thinks of as potentially threatening to his personal safety and, to a lesser degree, to others who are close to him.

A few examples will serve to show how these concerns have influenced the course of his life. He resigned his first position at an information desk in a bank when he was informed that he would be required to carry a hand gun. He has since then held a number of similar jobs which seem to him uncomplicated at the same time as they give him welcome contacts with the public. On his first visit to the U.S.A. he travelled by air both ways, but he announced shortly afterward that he would not come again unless he could travel by ship. He is nervous about riding in a car, especially on long trips in heavy traffic, but he accepts that risk when he wants to make the journey. On one occasion he was told that the spot on the shore on which he was standing would be under several feet of water in a few hours, and he wanted to leave the beach immediately. His eagerness to avoid involvement with the authorities has led him to become unusually well informed regarding the laws as they affect him and to be scrupulous in observing them.

P.S. had the ambition in his early years to become a Catholic priest, but circumstances beyond his control caused him to give up that goal. He completed his education through the public schools, roughly equivalent to the level attained after two years of college in America. He is single, lives with his parents, and feels responsible for doing so to look after their welfare. He is in my opinion (one shared by others who have come to know him well) above average intelligence but he cannot be characterised as an intellectual.

P.S. is extremely considerate of the feelings and rights of others in his dealings with them, and he expects the same treatment in return. In fact, he takes personal relations and commitments with the utmost seriousness, and some of his strongest disappointments in life are connected with incidents when he felt that persons did not conduct themselves toward him in a manner they had promised.

Everyone who becomes acquainted with P.S. sees him as a very friendly person, one who is the soul of courtesy. While he leads an outwardly simple life, such traits as those mentioned above make him inwardly complex.

If we ask why he has faithfully, and, apparently, tirelessly gone on in the same routine testing procedure when other subjects have become satiated in a much shorter period of time, we have to view the research against the background of what his life would have been without it. He once told me, when declining to fill in details about his youth, that there was nothing of interest to relate. He said that his life had been dull and had promised only more of the same until he began working as an ESP subject. This new activity has brought him not only the excitement of many visitors from abroad who clearly appreciated him and who told him many interesting things about the outside world. It has also made him widely known as a person with an ability that was of special scientific interest. To some extent he became a public figure within his own country, but P.S. always felt nervous about any attention that his work received at home. He preferred to work with scientists from outside his own country and also to have accounts of his work published abroad.

One of the most exciting moments of his life was during a visit that a colleague and I made in September, 1970. Earlier that year we had discovered that his picture and a brief account of his accomplishments had been included in *The Guinness Book of World Records,* where he was credited with holding the record for outstanding ESP performance. While he took great pride in having received this distinction abroad, he would be unhappy, I am sure, to have the fact become widely known in Prague.

On two other occasions his work was singled out as being worthy of special recognition, both times in a more scientific way. Twice the annual McDougall Award made to the scientist or scientists who published the most distinguished contribution to the literature of parapsychology during the year was given on the basis of research conducted with P.S. One of these times was early in the decade (1962) on the basis of work that Ryzl and I did together, and the other was seven years later (1969) for two research reports that Keil and I published. Combining all the impressions from these and other observations, I say with assurance that P.S. has a deep sense of the scientific importance of psi research and a strong feeling of pride regarding his own participation in it.

## REFERENCES

Anonymous. (1938) 'A scientist tests his own ESP ability.' *J. Parapsychol.,* **2,** 65–70

Beloff, J. (1968) 'ESP: Proof from Prague?' *New Scientist,* **40,** 76–77

Beloff, J., and Mandleberg, I. (1966) 'An attempted validation of the "Ryzl technique" for training ESP subjects.' *J.S.P.R.,* **43,** 229–249

Bender, H. (1936) *Zum Problem der Aussersinnlichen Wahrnehmung.* Johann Barth, Leipzig

Blom, J. G., and Pratt, J. G. (1968) 'A second confirmatory ESP experiment with Pavel Stepanek as a "borrowed" subject.' *J. Amer. S.P.R.,* **62,** 28–45

Drake, R. M. (1938) 'An unusual case of extra-sensory perception.' *J. Parapsychol.,* **2,** 184–198

Goldney, K. M., and Soal, S. G. (1938) 'Report on a series of experiments with Mrs. Eileen Garrett.' *Proc. S.P.R.,* **45,** 43–87

Haddox, V. (1966) 'A pilot study of a hypnotic method of training subjects in ESP.' *J. Parapsychol.,* **30,** 277–278 (Abstract)

Keil, H. H. J., and Pratt, J. G. (1969) 'Further ESP tests with Pavel Stepanek in Charlottesville dealing with the focusing effect.' *J. Amer. S.P.R.*, **63**, 253–272

Martin, D. R., and Stribic, F. P. (1938) 'Studies in extra-sensory perception: I. An analysis of 25 000 trials.' *J. Parapsychol.*, **2**, 23–30

Pegram, M. H. (1937) 'Some psychological relations of extra-sensory perception.' *J. Parapsychol.*, **1**, 191–205

Pratt, J. G. (1964) 'Preliminary experiments with a "borrowed" outstanding ESP subject.' *J.S.P.R.*, **42**, 333–345

Pratt, J. G. (1973) 'A decade of research with a selected ESP subject: an overview and reappraisal of the work with Pavel Stepanek.' *Proc. Amer. S.P.R.*, **30**, 1–78

Pratt, J. G., and Blom, J. G. (1964) 'A confirmatory experiment with a "borrowed" outstanding ESP subject.' *J.S.P.R.*, **42**, 381–389

Pratt, J. G., and Keil, H. H. J. (1969) 'The focusing effect as patterned behavior based on habitual object-word associations: a working hypothesis with supporting evidence.' *J. Amer. S.P.R.*, **63**, 314–337

Pratt, J. G., and Keil, H. H. J. (1972) 'Further consideration of the Stepanek focusing effect in the light of recent research findings.' *J. Amer. S.P.R.*, **66**, 345–356

Pratt, J. G., Keil, H. H. J., and Stevenson, I. (1970) 'Three-experimenter ESP tests of Pavel Stepanek during his 1968 visit to Charlottesville.' *J. Amer. S.P.R.*, **64**, 18–39

Pratt, J. G., and Ransom, C. (1972) 'Extrasensory perception or extraordinary sensory perception? A recent series of experiments with Pavel Stepanek.' *J. Amer. S.P.R.*, **66**, 63–85

Pratt, J. G., Rhine, J. B., Smith, B. M., Stuart, C. E., and Greenwood, J. A. (1940) *Extra-sensory perception after sixty years.* Holt, New York

Pratt, J. G., and Roll, W. G. (1968) 'Confirmation of the focusing effect in further ESP research with Pavel Stepanek in Charlottesville.' *J. Amer. S.P.R.*, **62**, 226–245

Pratt, J. G., Stevenson, I., Roll, W. G., Blom, J. G., Mcinsma, G. L., Keil, H. H. J., and Jacobson, N. (1968) 'Identification of concealed randomized objects through acquired response habits of stimulus and word association.' *Nature*, **220**, 89–91

Rhine, J. B. (1934a) *Extra-sensory perception.* Boston Society for Psychic Research, Boston

Rhine, J. B. (1934b) 'Telepathy and clairvoyance in the normal and trance states of a "medium".' *Character and Personality*, **3**, 91–111

Rhine, J. B. (1936) 'Some selected experiments in extra-sensory perception.' *J. Abnormal and Social Psychol.*, **31**, 216–228

Riess, B. F. (1937) 'A case of high scores in card guessing at a distance.' *J. Parapsychol.*, **1**, 260–263

Roll, W. G., and Pratt, J. G. (1968) 'An ESP test with aluminum cards.' *J. Amer. S.P.R.*, **62**, 381–386

Ryzl, M. (1962) 'Training the psi faculty by hypnosis.' *J.S.P.R.*, **41**, 234–252

Ryzl, M. (1966) 'A method of training in ESP.' *Int. J. Parapsychol.*, **8**, 501–532

Ryzl, M. (1968) 'Some observations on the mental impregnation hypothesis.' *Proc. Parapsychol. Assoc.*, No. 5.

Ryzl, M., Barendregt, J. T., Barkema, P. R., and Kappers, J. (1965) 'An experiment in Prague.' *J. Parapsychol.*, **29**, 176–184

Ryzl, M., and Pratt, J. G. (1962) 'Confirmation of ESP performance in a hypnotically prepared subject.' *J. Parapsychol.*, **26**, 237–243

Ryzl, M., and Pratt, J. G. (1963a) 'A further confirmation of stabilized ESP performance in a selected subject.' *J. Parapsychol.*, **27**, 73–83

Ryzl, M., and Pratt, J. G. (1963b) 'A repeated-calling ESP test with sealed cards.' *J. Parapsychol.*, **27**, 161–174

Ryzl, M., and Ryzlova, J. (1962) 'A case of high-scoring ESP performance in the hypnotic state.' *J. Parapsychol.*, **26**, 153–171

Soal, S. G., and Bateman, F. (1954) *Modern Experiments in Telepathy*. Yale, New Haven

Soal, S. G., and Bowden, H. T. (1959) *The Mind Readers*. Faber, London

Soal, S. G., and Goldney, K. M. (1943) 'Experiments in precognitive telepathy.' *Proc. S.P.R.*, **47**, 21–150

Stephenson, C. J. (1965) 'Cambridge ESP-hypnosis experiments (1958–64).' *J.S.P.R.*, **43**, 77–91

Warner, L. (1937) 'A test case.' *J. Parapsychol.*, **1**, 234–238

# 6 Modern Poltergeist Research—A Plea for an Unprejudiced Approach

**HANS BENDER**

## SYNOPSIS

*With this chapter we are confronted with phenomena of a different order of magnitude from any that we have previously encountered and accordingly we are forced to submit to an even greater strain on our credulity. The fastidious reader must be warned that this is very strong meat indeed. Faced with the bizarre array of gothic wonders which are here brought to light he may well wish to exclaim, in the words of the worthy gentleman whom the author quotes below: 'Did the sun of the Enlightenment shine in vain?'*

*The trail of the poltergeist is paved with booby-traps for the unwary and to tread it at all demands courage and a cool head. It is greatly to the credit of the author, Director of the Freiburg Institute and one of the only two individuals to hold a Chair in parapsychology at a European University,\* that he is not afraid to enter this treacherous terrain. Poltergeist research could be compared with an attempt to study electricity by observing only flashes of lightning! The typical poltergeist outbreak is of short duration and, by the time the investigator has arrived on the scene, the phenomena are likely to be already on the wane. To make matters worse, the publicity which such events usually attract in the press and the excitement they generate in the neighbourhood produce an atmosphere which is anything but conducive to serious scientific fieldwork. All too often, even if the phenomena were genuine to start with they become overlaid with the handiwork of hoaxers and practical jokers. There is, moreover, as the author explains, a kind of in-built elusiveness in the phenomena which makes them 'observer-shy'.*

*Nevertheless, we are not entirely helpless in this situation. Modern electronic technology which has made it notoriously easy to 'bug' the homes or offices of unsuspecting citizens can here be turned to*

\* The other is Dr Martin Johnson at the University of Utrecht.

*good advantage in tracking down the poltergeist and alerting us to what is going on. The Freiburg Institute have already availed themselves of these new monitoring facilities.*

*Yet, despite the fact that so many cases have been recorded and in such detail ever since the Middle Ages, the author admits that we are not much nearer to a proper understanding of the phenomena.*

*It is true that we no longer ascribe them to malicious spirits but the part played by the 'poltergeist focus' is anything but clear. Some theorists have gone so far as to suggest that there is a kind of psychic force emanating from the subject's body which is responsible for the effects observed. However, when one considers the amount of energy that is required—sometimes heavy articles of furniture are moved which the subject would be incapable of pushing or pulling using all his muscular strength—this seems somehow implausible. For my part, I think it more helpful to think of the subject as unleashing ordinary physical energy that is present in the environment to serve devious ends, rather as if a lightning conductor were able not merely to channel the path of the electric discharge but could somehow induce it out of the atmosphere. The author wisely refrains from committing himself on the theoretical issue but he does bring out clearly that the typical poltergeist phenomenon is not just an undirected release of energy, like an explosion, but is a controlled operation which, to all the world, looks like the work of invisible hands.*

*Poltergeists have become all the more important to parapsychology since the virtual disappearance of physical mediumship. The astonishing incidents which surround the young Annemarie during the now famous Rosenheim case, which is here described at some length, are in some ways reminiscent of the sort of things that were reported from the séances of Eusapia Palladino or others of her like during the heyday of Spiritualism. There are even some indications that certain mediums began their careers as poltergeist children. It has been the author's hope to be able to tame the poltergeist powers by converting their human focus into a serviceable special subject for experimental parapsychology though, so far, his efforts in this direction have been largely frustrated. But, whether Annemarie is to be regarded as an incipient physical medium or a latter day witch, there is a nice sense of modernity in her choice of her employer's telephone system and electrical appliances as the target of her witchcraft:*

*Although the Freiburg Institute has investigated some 35 alleged poltergeist outbreaks since the War, the author rightly gives pride of place to the Rosenheim case, not only because of the spectacular or fantastic nature of the phenomena but because a variety of circumstances combined to make it one of the most evidential of modern times which has had a far-reaching effect on German public opinion. For, it was not just parapsychologists who were eager to get to the bottom of this mystery but also the post office authorities and telephone engineers, the municipal power station and, last but not least, the police! In addition the services of two physicists from the prestigious Max Planck Institute were called upon and both were baffled and impressed.*

*Bender continues his survey with two more recent cases from the files of the Freiburg Institute, the Pursruck case of 1970–71 and the Scherfede case of 1972–73. In both of these the role of poltergeist focus seems to have been filled by a pubescent girl but, whereas the Pursruck case is, relatively speaking, a routine affair with the archetypal noises and knockings which the word 'poltergeist' originally suggested, the Scherfede case is In a class apart, involving as it does the paranormal displacement of large quantities of water. A 'water-poltergeist' is a very great rarity in the literature—Owen (1964) lists only a few such cases, mainly from late nineteenth century America— so any poltergeist fancier can account himself lucky to have come across even one such case. If, as the author maintains, no natural explanation can be found for the extraordinary happenings he describes in this connection then, in its flagrant and anarchic violation of natural law, it exceeds anything we have had to reckon with in this book.*

*The trail of the poltergeist, as I have already remarked, is beset with untold obstacles and hazards. Whether, as the author suggests, it will also prove in the end to be the royal road to an enlargement of our understanding of ourselves and our universe is a point which must be left to the reader to ponder.*

*Editor*

In his most informative book *Can we explain the Poltergeist?* A. R. G. Owen explains the origin of the German word 'poltergeist', which is now more commonly used in English than in my own language. The word means a 'noise spirit' and was current in Germany in Reformation times, being used by Luther to describe a noisy, racketing type of demon (Owen, 1964). In a classic of poltergeist literature *The Night-Side of Nature* of 1848 (cited in Sitwell, 1940), Catherine Crowe included a chapter 'The Poltergeist of the Germans' which later served as a basis to formulate the definition of poltergeist activity as employed by Andrew Lang and Frank Podmore.

Owen adopted the definition which seemed acceptable to Lang and Podmore and states it as follows:

> 'Poltergeist activity is the occurrence of one or both of the following, taking place in an apparently spontaneous but often sporadic way:
>
> a. Production of noises, e.g. tappings, sawings, bumpings.
> b. Movement of objects by no known physical means.'

As Owen shows in his book, the poltergeist is actually a much more complex phenomenon. But these basic features may do for the introduction to this paper in which I will comment on some new German poltergeist cases.

## THE BARRIER OF PREJUDICE

Poltergeist phenomena are still highly controversial. Antagonists of psi regard them as the peak of superstitious beliefs. Adherents—laymen and scientists—who accept unexplainable occurrences in the realm of extrasensory perception often seem reluctant to include in their positive attitude the reality of events which affect the sanctified laws regulating the behaviour of physical objects. This reluctance does not date from modern times. As I pointed out in my Presidential Address to the Parapsychological Association (Bender, 1969), it has a long history and seems to be rooted in some basic personality structure. There have always been 'goats' and 'sheep', disbelievers and believers, in regard to the paranormal and especially to physical phenomena. I need only cite Joseph Glanvil, one of the first members of the Royal Society who, in 1666, began his famous report on a poltergeist case by saying he knew very well '. . . that the present day world treats all such stories with laughter and derision and is firmly convinced they should be scorned as a waste of time and old wives' tales . . .' (Glanvil, 1721).

Although reported through the centuries, poltergeist phenomena have always been in the twilight of delusion and fraudulent manipulation. Trickery, bad observation, hallucinations have been mentioned as plausible causes for the alleged poltergeist outrages. The reports were scorned. Andrew Lang's courageous breakthrough was walled up again by a generation of disbelievers who put forward the 'naughty little girl' theory or suggested that earth movements due to subsidence, underground water, or to tidal action cause movements of the structure of buildings, and therefore noises and possibly movement of objects inside the buildings.

C. G. Jung, the famous Swiss psychologist, struck at these kinds of generalised, evasive statements when he wrote in the preface to Fanny Moser's book *Spuk*: 'The prejudice dominating in many places in regard to the factual reports here in question shows all the symptoms of a primitive fear of ghosts. Even educated people who should be better informed, use occasionally the most absurd arguments, become illogical and deny the testimony of their own senses' (Moser, 1950).

The prejudice against poltergeist phenomena can be overcome only by an impartial scientific investigation of a problem which seems to be as old as mankind. The Poltergeist is a challenge for scientists and one which parapsychologists, after a long period of purely laboratory experimentation, are beginning to accept. The lifting of the taboo was accompanied by a new change in nomenclature: poltergeists which, according to Jung, seem to arouse a fear of spirits, are now neutralised by the scientific name of 'Recurrent Spontaneous Psychokinesis' (RSPK). There is no question any more of such a thing as a 'poltergeist' existing as an entity and capable of manifesting independently of any human 'focus'. In 34 of 35 cases which the Freiburg Institute investigated since 1948—some at first-hand, some at second-hand—the poltergeist focus has been an identifiable human being, generally a youngster. Thus, defence mechanisms against a frightening world of demons seem unnecessary. Only one of our cases was that of a classical 'haunted house'. Visual and acoustical phenomena, as well as displacement of objects, had been observed for a period of 60 years. I admit it is difficult to cope with cases of this kind as they show but little analogy to what we observe in our experimental laboratory research.

## PATTERNS OF POLTERGEIST OCCURRENCES

Unexplainable incidents of a physical nature have been reported for centuries with a remarkable uniformity. A survey of historical cases in comparison with modern ones can be found in Moser (1950), Owen (1964), Thurston (1954) and others. Striking similarities in the cases observed throughout the centuries in all countries are emphasised by these authors, especially by Owen. An analysis of recurrent patterns in recent reports of poltergeist phenomena has been undertaken by the French police officer Emile Tizané. His work (Tizané, 1951), is based on a great number of cases of alleged poltergeist events investigated by the French police between 1925 and 1950. Among the uniform patterns Tizané found in comparing the independent reports I call special attention to the following:

a. Bombardment. Often a house becomes the object of a real hail of projectiles. Stones fall on the roof, break panes, and penetrate through openings. Phenomena rarely occur in the interior of the house once outside bombardment from the exterior begins.

b. Bangs against doors, the walls, or the furniture are heard, sometimes at the same place and sometimes in all parts of the house.

c. Doors, windows and even securely closed cupboards open by themselves.

d. Objects are skilfully displaced or thrown. Fragile ones are often unbroken, even after a jump of several feet while solid ones are sometimes completely destroyed.

e. Bizarre cracks and noises are sometimes observed.

f. Displaced objects sometimes do not show a 'regular' trajectory. They behave as if they had been transported and may even follow the contours of furniture.

g. In some rare instances, foreign objects penetrate into a closed space.

h. When handled by observers, the objects give a sensation of being warm.

i. Objects seem to form themselves in the air.

I lay special stress on the oddity of the phenomena in question precisely because they have an extremely important bearing on the problem of how we can explain the poltergeist and come up with a workable theory. They represent a sort of counterpoise to the carefully investigated analogies of RSPK with familiar energetic processes which Artley and Roll (1971) have recently described. Their analysis suggested that the energy responsible for the occurrences was attentuated with distance and that there had been a conversion of psi energy to kinetic energy. An exponential decay curve was found to fit the data best. This stems from the Seaford case which was investigated by Pratt and Roll (1958). Like the later Newark and Miami cases, which were investigated by the same team, it did *not* show any of the 'oddities' of Tizané's list. There was nothing unusual about the trajectory of the objects. Thus, there was no suggestion that they turned corners; the landing place of an object was always consistent with a straight motion from its point of origin. There was no penetration or 'tele-apportation' into a closed space, nor formation of objects in the air, etc. Obviously, there are various types of poltergeist incidents, and we do not yet have the slightest idea whether different forms of 'psi energy'—if there is such a thing—are involved, or only one and the same psi process with different manifestations. All we can actually do in search of a theory is to review the variety of patterns that we find reported from all over the world and in all ages and try our best to assess their authenticity.

## SUGGESTIONS FOR THE INVESTIGATION OF POLTERGEIST PHENOMENA

In both ongoing and retrospective cases the first concern of the investigators is, of course, to find out if the alleged phenomena are suggestive or not of RSPK. Alleged poltergeist phenomena may simply be due to a misinterpretation of a natural cause: in one of our cases loud thumps accompanied by vibrations of the walls of a little house were found to be stemming from a defect of the water pipes. Deliberate trickery in the beginning of alleged poltergeist cases seems to be rarer than the 'naughty little girl' theory supposes. But as a matter of fact it happens rather often in the course of the investigation of a genuine case when scientists with tape recorders and cameras are eagerly expecting phenomena and are slowly losing patience. The transition from unconsciously produced genuine phenomena to trickery often seems to stem from the same motivational source: the trend to hoax as a form of aggressive discharge of inner tensions. Semiconscious or unconscious fraud is sometimes to be found in cases in which hysterical persons are involved, who in a pathological state similar to that of sleep-walking, induce poltergeist-like phenomena.

In most of the 35 cases investigated by the Freiburg Institute it was easy to determine the 'poltergeist focus', usually an adolescent. The phenomena seem to be connected with the presence of the focus person and to occur in his vicinity. This raises the problem of distance, a still rather obscure topic of RSPK research. In the well known Rosenheim case there is fairly good evidence that PK phenomena happened in the lawyer's office when an employee, Annemarie Sch., the undoubted focus, was 1500 yards away. Some cases seem to indicate an unconscious co-operation of two persons, e.g. mother and child or sisters as in the Pursruck case which I will describe later. If it is not obvious who is the focus, systematic elimination of the persons involved in the poltergeist events may help to determine the relevant person.

As to witnesses' statements it goes without saying that a perfect agreement may be due to a 'fable convenue' or confabulation, that is, by relating over and over again the astonishing phenomena, a certain version gets itself adopted. If there was any suspicion of a 'fable convenue', I found it helpful to reconstruct the alleged phenomena by the use of photographs and/or film with a view to controlling the witnesses' statements. The reaction to the reconstruction as shown by the individual witnesses may be most informative for their original observations.

Objective documents, taped and filmed records of poltergeist occurrences, are highly desirable but difficult to obtain. We use television cameras, videotape recorders, etc., to monitor the situations where poltergeist phenomena may possibly show up. A laboratory on wheels, a Volkswagen-Bus, serves for the instalment of the supervising devices. Thus we try to elude as far as possible a disturbance of the spontaneous display of the phenomena by visible technical arrangements. So far, we have had but little success in obtaining objective recordings but in the end, we did succeed in videotaping the sudden rotation of a painting in the Rosenheim case and also in detecting the trick of a 10 year old youngster who, after producing what was almost certainly genuine PK phenomena, had become a 'naughty little girl' who threw objects and broke panes. Incidentally, an objective documentation of genuine events and of trickery has to cope with the same difficulties. Needless to say, the evidential value of taped or filmed records of poltergeist occurrences is entirely dependent on the integrity of the experimenters.

If a poltergeist case seems to show matter through matter penetration, the technique of sealing the boxes and cupboards into which or out of which objects are alleged to move can be reinforced by using light responsive photo-electric switches acting on a release which triggers photo or film cameras or videotape recorders. The ideal instrument to control the trajectory of objects which are said to come out of closed spaces would be a high frequency camera yielding up to 10 000 shots per second. Documents of this kind would perhaps enable us to discuss on an empirical basis the hypothesis that penetrating objects have been dematerialised and then rematerialised—a somewhat artifical postulate which, of course, has no background in established physical laws.

Attempts to provoke poltergeist occurrences through posthypnotic suggestion of the presumed focus person have not yet been successful in our investigations. In some cases it was not possible to induce a deep hypnotic trance in the subject, in others we had to respect the wish of the parents to abstain from any measures which could alter the subject's state of consciousness. However, the method is promising as Dr Bjerre's success in the Karin case shows (Bjerre, 1947).

Poltergeist cases should always be analysed in terms of a 'field theory': the interaction between the focus person and the social situation in which the poltergeist phenomena show up has to be carefully studied with a view to an understanding of the motivation underlying PK phenomena. This analysis implies, of course, a study of the personality structure of the subject with appropriate methods such as life data, test data of various kinds and questionnaire data (Mischo, 1958).

In all cases where laboratory experimentation with the subjects was possible, we found highly significant ESP scoring but could not elicit experimental PK.

## A CHANGE OF ATTITUDE TOWARDS POLTERGEIST PHENOMENA IN WESTERN GERMANY

At the end of the fifties, an Institute for Public Opinion Research, in collaboration with the Freiburg Institute, undertook a representative Gallup poll on the attitude of Western German adults towards poltergeist phenomena and haunted houses. It was learned that 72% of the adult population hold that such alleged phenomena are pure superstition. Eighteen per cent are convinced that these strange things really happen and the remaining 10% have no opinion. This distribution proved not to be stable. When the Rosenheim poltergeist case and the result of our investigation in collaboration with physicists became known, the percentage of believers rose by 10% to 28% in Bavaria, where regional television broadcasts were aired. In the meantime, it had become widely known that the investigation of the Rosenheim poltergeist case had been sponsored by the *Deutsche Forschungsgemeinschaft* (German Association for the Advancement of Science), an official body which subsidises research. This fact contributed to overcoming public reluctance to accept research of this kind. Thus, the Rosenheim case became a kind of 'breakthrough' for an unprejudiced attitude towards RSPK phenomena in Western Germany and other German speaking countries. An analysis of other special circumstances, both parapsychological and sociological, may be helpful in understanding this change of attitude.


## THE ROSENHEIM CASE 1967–68

At the end of November, 1967, inexplicable events were reported in the German press to be taking place in a lawyer's office in the Bavarian town of Rosenheim. Electric bulbs exploded, neon lights attached to a ceiling 2·5 metres high went out time and again. Electricians found them unscrewed from their sockets by about 90 degrees. Sharp bangs were reported, automatic fuses were said to have blown without cause, and developing fluid in photostatic copying machines spilled many times. The work of the lawyer's office was severely impaired by telephone disturbances which had already been observed in the previous summer: the four telephones often rang simultaneously, conversations were cut short and the telephone bills rose to an unusual height.

The lawyer and his personnel suspected disturbances in the power supply as the cause of the strange occurrences. The maintenance department of the municipal power station and the post office authorities started a thorough investigation: monitoring equipment was introduced to measure fluctuations in the power supply and an automatic counter installed which registered number, time and length for every call made in the office. The monitoring instruments registered large deflections that sometimes appeared simultaneously with the abnormal phenomena and persisted even when—as a last trial to exclude undetectable causes in the general power system—an emergency power unit was installed to ensure 'undisturbed' electric current in the lawyer's office. The counter of the post office registered innumerable calls of the time announcement number (0119), often dialled six times a minute and this for weeks.

The Bavarian and the General Western German Television produced broadcasts about this unusual case by the end of November, 1967, which since then have become almost historic documents. They show the destructions in the lawyer's office, the instalment of the monitoring equipment, the statements of the perplexed technicians, the plaints of the lawyer and the authoritarian affirmation of an official of the post office that this perfect organisation is always capable of detecting disturbances and that the 0119 calls must have been dialled in the office. The employees denied having done the calling.

The broadcast ended with the open question: Are the strange occurrences due to a technical defect or to mischief? But who could be interested in such continued practical jokes? This was the situation when, on December 1st, 1967, the Freiburg Institute began its investigation.

Figure 6.1    Annemarie Sch. Investigators from the Freiberg Institute concluded that the poltergeist phenomena exhibited in the Rosenheim Case were connected with Annemarie.

We found that only during office hours did the unusual phenomena and deflections of the monitoring instruments occur. A first deflection was often registered at the very minute when Annemarie Sch. (*see* Figure 6.1), a 19 year old employee, crossed the threshold of the office in the morning. When this young girl walked through the gangways, the lamps behind her began to swing with increasing amplitude (*see* Figure 6.2). If bulbs exploded, the

Figure 6.2    Photograph of the swinging lamps in the lawyer's offices. The phenomenon only occurred during office hours when the secretary Annemarie Sch. was in the building.

fragments flew towards her. In addition, the number of phenomena decreased with increasing distance from Miss Sch. It became obvious that we were dealing with RSPK connected with Annemarie.

We had first to rule out the hypothesis of disturbances in the power supply. Two physicists, Dr F. Karger and Dipl. Phys. G. Zicha from the Max Planck Institute for Plasmaphysics in Munich, observed and examined the recorder deflections and systematically eliminated or checked every conceivable physical cause. They could definitely prove that the anomalous deflections were not caused by mains voltage rises. They came to the following conclusions:

1. Although recorded with the facilities available to experimental physics, the phenomena defy explanation with the means available to theoretical physics.
2. The phenomena seem to be the result of non-periodic, short duration forces.
3. The phenomena (including the telephone incidents) do not seem to involve pure electrodynamic effects.
4. Not only do simple events of an explosive type take place, but also complicated motions (e.g. recorder curves, moving pictures).
5. The movements seem to be performed by intelligently controlled forces (e.g. the telephone incidents) that have a tendency to evade investigation.

The discovery of the PK nature of the occurrences led to an intensification of the events: paintings began to swing and to turn, drawers came out by themselves, documents were displaced, a 175 kilogram cabinet moved twice about 30 cm from the wall, etc. Annemarie Sch., getting more and more nervous, finally displayed hysterical contractions in her arms and legs. When she was sent on leave, nothing happened, and when she definitely left the office for a new position, no more disturbances occurred. But similar events, less obvious and kept secret, happened for some time in the new office where she was working (cf. Bender, 1968 and 1969, Karger and Zicha, 1968).

The Rosenheim case involved about forty first-hand witnesses who were thoroughly interrogated, among them technicians, the criminal police (lawyer Adam had placed an accusation against the unknown), physicians, journalists, clients of the office whose testimonies could be compared with our own observations. The final result of the investigation was broadcast by Western German Television. The controlled publicity of the case, the shift from a misleading technical interpretation to the PK evidence which could be followed up by millions of spectators led to the breakthrough in public opinion.

## THE PURSRUCK CASE 1970–71

The changed attitude towards poltergeist phenomena became symptomatically manifest in the behaviour of the catholic priest, Rev. Jakob Wolfsteiner, who is in charge of the pastoral duties in the small village of Pursruck, 40 miles east of Nuremberg. In November 1970 two girls, Helga, 13, and Anna R., 11, were living for some time with their grandmother in a former old schoolhouse. After a resident of the ground floor of this building had died, tappings and bumpings were heard. Disturbing noises continued for about three weeks. Each resident of the house accused the others of producing the noise.

At the end of May, 1971, the tappings began again. In addition scrapes and sawings were heard when the two girls went to bed, about 8 p.m. The noise seemed to come from the beds, but also from cupboards and doors. It was like the hammering of a machine gun interrupted by intense bangs. The same phenomena showed in the house of the girls' parents, and the knocking was even heard in the street. The family felt terribly disturbed. As the noises seemed to come from the beds, hammocks were arranged for the girls in a special room in the hope that the tapping would now come to an end. But the noise continued, now in the form of a scratching.

Everyone in the region knew about the phenomena and people got more and more excited. Some spoke of 'witchcraft' and nailed twigs against the door in order to drive away the evil spirits, others thought of practical jokes, scolding the two girls for their cheeky tricks. Newspapers were full of suppositions, water diviners pretended to discover underground water-courses which they declared to be the answer to the riddle. In this phase a student from Freiburg registered the tappings on a tape recorder. He found that they were strongest when the two girls were together in bed, less strong when Helga was alone, and quite low, when only Anna lay down.

As the excitement about the phenomena kept growing, Rev. Wolfsteiner took the two girls with their parents to his parsonage in Lintach, a place next to Pursruck. The two girls lay down on a wooden table, and the tappings immediately began. Knockings were also heard when they stretched themselves out on the carpet in the parsonage, as many witnesses testify. All these phenomena were tape recorded. From the pulpit Rev. Wolfsteiner declared that there was no reason to believe in demonic influences. He declared that a new science, parapsychology, examined such phenomena called 'psychokinesis' and explained that they can unconsciously be produced by certain persons. Scientific investigation, he continued, had to exclude fraud. He announced experimental research into this case and proceeded to personal observations. He presented a report of his research to the Freiburg Institute. The following extract shows that he worked like a well trained parapsychologist:

> 'In the evening of June 19th, 1971, I went to Pursruck with the agreement of the parents and the children of the family R. I took along my Contaflex camera with long distance objective, an electric flashlight, and a tape recorder. The girls were in their beds. In the first minutes, they were covered with their blankets, holding their hands folded on their foreheads. Later on, the girls' father took away the blankets so that their feet and their whole body could be seen. Tappings were to be heard. I took about 16 flashlight photographs which can be controlled on the tape, as the closure of the camera can clearly be recognized with each photograph. At first I took the flashlight snapshots in the dark. Then I observed the girls in the light of an electric torch. Tappings appeared when the girls lay completely quiet in their beds and went on when I spoke to them. After these observations I was definitely convinced that the girls could not possibly have caused the phenomena with their hands or other parts of their bodies.'

Rev. Wolfsteiner had, previous to this experiment, called Father Dr A. Heimler, psychotherapist, for help in observation and therapy. Father Heimler made the children execute rhythmical dances in order to relax them and succeeded in calming their anxiety. His report, too, is a document of the changed attitude towards poltergeist phenomena. I want to cite a few passages:

> 'It seems that the poltergeist (the unconscious) reacts directly to hot rhythms and answers, at least partially, according to the beat music of the "Manhattan" and to the clapping of the "Spare-Hully-Gully".'

> 'The noises cannot be exactly localized. They mostly seem to come from the beds in which the girls are lying. It is obvious that the kind of support determines the type of noise. When the support is smooth and elastic—i.e. when the girls are sleeping in the hammocks—there is only a scratching to be heard. When a board is put into the hammocks, a tapping appears. However, these noises can also come from a distant cupboard door.

Once, the cupboard door opened with a loud bang and glasses in the cupboard fell to the ground from the vibration and broke into pieces.'

The phenomena, Dr Heimler points out in his report, appeared for the first time on the day following the death of a resident of the old school house. Helga, who looked from her window directly over the cemetery and the mortuary where the corpse had been taken, was frightened and could not fall alseep. She was thinking of a ghost story which her teacher had told months ago. When she first heard the tappings, she thought that the dead man was announcing himself in this way. Then she discarded this inter-pretation and thought, just like her sister Anna and her grand-mother, that the dead man's wife was beating out her blankets in the night. The second poltergeist period at the end of May 1971 was preceded by anxiety dreams which clearly showed puberty problems (a man standing in her bed is threatening her with vipers). Father H. concludes his report with the remarks:

'The phenomena are certainly not sufficiently explained by puberty crises . . . It remains a riddle, why these tensions could discharge themselves in paranormal effects and not in another way . . . In the Pursruck case they ought to be regarded as a public appeal to humanitarian understanding as well as a challenge for considering the reality of the paranormal.'

The pioneer work of the two priests had perfectly prepared the investigation of the case by the Freiburg Institute. When we arrived on the spot, the phenomena were still going on. We succeeded in making videotape recordings while the girls were in bed and the tappings appeared in different intensity. Rapid knockings, raps and heavy bangs could be registered. One heard Helga saying 'I am so frightened'. The father reported an observa-tion which frightened him in his turn: alarmed by the tapping phenomena, the girls came to their parents' beds. Mr R. rose and saw that suddenly the bedside rug rolled up 'all by itself'. We rearranged this situation and filmed it.

Once the paranormal origin of the tapping phenomena was established, we lifted for a while our controlling measures in order to get a more detached climate. We suggested asking questions to the 'tapping spirit'—as the phenomenon was jokingly called. The girls should begin to ask for the number of persons present and slowly proceed to easy arithmetic tasks. Our interest in this experiment was therapeutic as well as scientific: the girls should assume an active determined attitude towards the phenomenon in order to overcome their anxiety. They accepted this idea with enthusiasm, but when we, again, applied more strict controls, it became obvious that they cheated by knocking with toes or fingers against the bedstead. Questioned, they first looked for excuses, but then admitted their fraud. Our measure had its therapeutic success. The frightening side of the phenomena was somewhat banished for them, but for the investigation of the paranormal aspect it meant a short circuit. We invited the children for a recreation holiday in the Black Forest; they were taken care of by clinical psychologists. ESP tests brought a slightly positive result. In August, the parents informed us about new phenomena, but it could not be cleared if they were genuine or fraudulent. A new experimental supervision yielded no positive results.

Of course, the change of attitude which became obvious in the Pursruck case is not a general one. There are still fanatic disbelievers which by their affective statements against the paranormal give away their own complexes. Thus, a public prosecutor wrote in an article 'The Curious Science of Poltergeist Professors' (Kriminalistik, July 1970); 'As a matter of fact, there is a close connection between the disgusting and bloody superstitious belief in witches and parapsychology. We are sick of the cadaverous smell that professors of old blew into our nostrils with their atrocity stories . . . Did the sun of the Enlightenment shine in vain?' We often cite this remarkable statement as an example of negative superstition.

## THE SCHERFEDE CASE 1972–73

In the last days of 1972, the magistrate of the administrative district Warburg-Land in Westphalia, 25 miles west of Kassel, applied to the Freiburg Institute for an investigation of mysterious water phenomena which had occurred for several weeks in Scherfede, a big village of 3000 inhabitants. The phenomena began in September 1972 in one of the small houses of a settlement which a building society had erected at the end of the fifties. Small puddles of water appeared first in the bathroom, then in the kitchen and in other rooms. Mechanics checked the water pipes and the heating tubes but could not find any leakage. In October and November humid spots showed on the walls, carpets became wet but the underlying structures proved to be dry. Pools of water also appeared outside the house and several times the outer walls were wet. It looked like the splash of a watering can or a pipe. A technician in charge of the water supply of the village, checked time and again without being able to find the slightest hint where the water could come from.

A dramatic escalation began on December 10th. In intervals of 20–30 minutes, big water puddles appeared in the drawing room of the house. The family K.—father, mother and a 13-year-old girl Kerstin—heard a splashing when they were in another room. Nothing happened when they were present, and no one has ever seen a pool in formation. Technicians came and admitted that they were completely puzzled and could not find any cause. Trickery was excluded by carefully observing the room in question. At 7.30 p.m. neighbours of the next but one house came and asked for help: floods of water had suddenly appeared on the second floor and were coming down the staircase. There was too much to mop up with floor cloths. Helpers formed an echelon and brushed it out of the house. They were still at work when an hour later help was claimed for the next house where unexplainable water pools and splashes appeared and, another hour later, the same happened in the adjoining house, the last one of the row. This continued, more or less intensely, for three days.

The technicians cut off the water at the main in the first house, of the family K., but water pools and splashes appeared nevertheless. A probe was taken and examined in a chemical laboratory of Paderborn which was in charge of the routine supervision of Scherfede's water supply. It proved to be identical with the water of Scherfede's springs. Experts were brought into play, building technicians, geologists and hydrologists. They were unable to find any rational cause for these flabbergasting events and finally advised the local authorities and the magistrate of the administrative district to apply to the Freiburg Institute as they all had heard of the Rosenheim and Pursruck cases. In the meantime the newspapers reported on the 'water poltergeist' of Scherfede and the witnesses were presented in a television broadcast.

The Freiburg team arrived on January 4th, 1973. The last phenomenon had happened in December, 1972, in the house where the occurrences originated. We were told that firemen of Scherfede were posted as guards in the house K. One of them had observed that in the very moment when for a while he turned his head, a pool of water had appeared on the floor of the kitchen.

We explored many witnesses, photographed the traces of the water disaster in the different houses and could easily discern the direction of splashes on the furniture and other forms of the water invasion: big spots on the ceilings and walls and distorted wooden bars of the parquet floor.

Fantastic hypotheses about the cause of the amazing phenomena circulated in Scherfede. A number of people connected them with the construction of a new highway-bridge near to the houses, and thought of the pressure of underground water, others supposed that gases in the room condensed to water. Some older people remembered that the territory belonged to the church and supposed demonic influences. Right from the beginning of our research we were confronted with whispered hunches that the water disaster had to do with the 13 year old daughter Kerstin of the family K. We followed them up and found that Kerstin used to go to the lavatory in other houses. In two cases it had been observed that a water pool showed when Kerstin had used the lavatory. In the house of a fireman, near to the houses of the settlement, a water pool had once appeared when Kerstin came from the toilet. One of the families which later on had to suffer during the escalation—which lasted from December 10th to December 14th—forbade her to enter their house. Kerstin had never used the toilet of the house adjacent to that of her parents. The two families were not on good terms. Nothing happened in this house.

It was difficult to interrogate Kerstin. Both she and her parents were reluctant to allow personal interviews. We were asked why we concentrated on her and did not pay the same attention to others. She reacted to a first interview with tears, and we could not apply the whole battery of psychodiagnostic tests which we had prepared for her. But we succeeded in tranquilising her and the parents and did our utmost to keep our suspicion secret that she is the 'poltergeist focus'. An open agreement with the whispers in the village would have been a burden for her and the family. We hope to continue the clinical analysis of the case which already shows hints in the direction of what the German psychoanalyst Schultz-Henke calls an 'urethral neurosis', a syndrome characterised by a desire to dominate on the basis of an ego-weakness.

Under these circumstances our conclusion that the water occurrences are psi events probably dependent on the girl Kerstin was confidentially given to the authorities who had applied to us and made known in public only in a general way.

The Scherfede case presents many interesting features. The most striking one is for me the matter through matter penetration which seems to be involved. The analyses of the probes showed that the pools are tap water. It is most likely that it came out of the water pipes or the heating system with its boiler. If we had been present during the three days when the phenomenon was escalating we should have stained the water in the water-pipes with a methylene blue dye and the water in the heating system with 'eosine', a special red dye. Another striking feature is the distance in regard to the probable focus Kerstin. She was not present in the houses where successively the phenomena showed. The last house is about 300 metres away from her residence. The phenomena do not show any sign of attenuation implied by Artley and Roll (1971) with their concept of an 'exponential decay curve', indicating a spatiotemporal correlation between a person and the disturbances. In this case I cannot find the slightest hint of a 'conversion of psi energy to kinetic energy' as these authors suggest as fitting their own data best.

In the sociological context the Scherfede case presents another example for the change of attitude towards unexplainable phenomena in the physical world: the widespread information on poltergeist events induces official authorities to apply for a parapsychological investigation.

It looked like a meaningful coincidence that returning home from Scherfede, I found on my desk an issue of the Italian magazine *Annabella* with an article 'in questo bambino c'è il demonio?' (Is this child possessed by the devil?)—the story of a 9 year old boy who, hospitalised with a virus hepatitis in the clinic San Francesco in Nuoro (Sardinia) 'made water spout from the floor and knocked pieces of furniture down without touching them'. This happened at the end of November, 1972. The article cites the director of the clinic, Prof. Giuseppe Marras, who stated: 'The phenomenon of the water splashes on the floor is genuine. There is no doubt. I have seen it with my own eyes. I understand that people ask for an explanation, but I must confess that I cannot give any. Shall I speak of psychokinesis, parapsychology and things like that? I could do it but you know that this new branch of science cannot explain it either'. Other cases of unexplainable water occurrences have been reported. It would be rewarding to follow up thoroughly this pattern of RSPK.

The increasing interest in psi phenomena in my country, which was partly stimulated by the exciting reports in the mass media on scientifically investigated RSPK cases, led to public discussions with leading physicists. Thus—to give an example—the Catholic

Academy of the Archbishop of Freiburg twice invited representatives of theoretical and experimental physics for panel discussions with parapsychologists. Wolfgang Büchel (Bochum), Helmut Hönl (Freiburg), Pascual Jordan (Hamburg), Jürgen Petzold (Marburg), all well known professors of physics, and Friedbert Karger (Max Planck Institute for Plasmaphysics in Munich) admitted ESP and PK as facts and as a challenge for their science. No model of reasoning could be offered for an integration of psi in the actual frame of the natural sciences, and in regard to RSPK and PK, it was widely discussed whether phenomena in the material world which happen in connection with psychic events would ever become an object for physics as science of matter.

Let me terminate with two of the final statements the physicists gave on the panel discussion. Prof. Jordan said:

'If we estimate the psi phenomenon of the so called "clairvoyance" type as real, it would be almost inconsistent in terms of physics to doubt in principle the possibility of PK, for it is one of the most general and profound of all basic laws of physics that every action is accompanied by a corresponding reaction. If there is a paranormal influence on states of the mind by objective events of the outer world in the form of clairvoyance, then it is logical to assume that conversely an influence of psychic forces on material objects of the outer world exists.'

Dr Karger said:

'We have investigated with particular intensity a case of RSPK. This was the Rosenheim case, 1967. In the course of this investigation we came to the conclusion that it cannot be explained by the means of today's theoretical physics. On the other hand we ascertained its existence by means of the same experimental physics. I cannot offer any model which seems to fit these phenomena. That they really do exist could be established with the utmost certainty.'

Poltergeist phenomena are, I believe, a *via regia* or royal road to an extended understanding of man, of his position in nature and of nature herself. The time has surely come to abandon our antiquated prejudices.

## REFERENCES

Artley, J. L., and Roll, W. G. (1971) 'Mathematical Models and the Attentuation Effect in Two RSPK (Poltergeist) Cases.' *Proc. of the Parapsychol. Assoc., No. 5*, 29–31

Bender, H. (1968) 'An Investigation of "Poltergeist" Occurrences.' *Proc. of the Parapsychol. Assoc.*, No. 5, 31–33

Bender, H. (1969) 'New Developments in Poltergeist Research.' Presidential Address, Twelfth Annual Convention of the Parapsychological Association, New York City, September 5, 1969. *Proc. of the Parapsychol. Assoc.*, No. 6, 81–102

Bjerre, P. (1947) *Spökerier.* Centrum, Stockholm

Glanvil, J. (1721) *Sadducismus Triumphatus, or, A Full and Plain Evidence Concerning Witches and Apparitions.* In two parts, 4th edition, London

Karger, F., and Zicha, G. (1967) 'Physical Investigation of Psychokinetic Phenomena in Rosenheim, Germany, 1967.' *Proc. of the Parapsychol. Assoc.*, No. 5, 33–35

Mischo, J. (1958) 'Personality Structure of Psychokinetic Mediums.' *Proc. of the Parapsychol. Assoc.*, No. 5, 35–37

Moser, F. (1950) *Spuk. Irrglaube oder Wahrglaube?* Preface by C. G. Jung. Baden bei Zurich

Owen, A. R. G. (1964) *Can we explain the Poltergeist?* Garrett Publications, New York

Pratt, J. G., and Roll, W. G. (1958) 'The Seaford Disturbances.' *J. Parapsychol.*, **22**, 79–124

Roll, W. G. (1972) *The Poltergeist,* Nelson Doubleday, New York (1972) and New American Library PB, New York (1973)

Sitwell, S. (1940) *Poltergeists.* Faber, London

Thurston, H. (1954) *Ghosts and Poltergeists.* Henry Regnery, Chicago

Tizané, E. (1951) *Sur la Piste de l'Homme Inconnu. Les Phénomènes de Hantise et de Possession.* Paris

# 7 A New Look at the Survival Problem*

## W. G. ROLL

## SYNOPSIS

*There are many contemporary philosophers who regard the concept of personal identity as so inextricably bound up with the identity of the body as to consider it doubtful whether it even makes sense to talk of disembodied existence. The author, however, takes his point of departure from the late C. D. Broad, the eminent Cambridge philosopher, who, in common with the generality of mankind, had no difficulty in conceding the logical possibility of surving his own bodily death and who even thought that there was sufficient empirical evidence to make such a supposition plausible. As a pessimist about the human condition and an agnostic Broad did not relish the prospect but, as a philosopher, his principal concern was how best to conceptualise such a state of being.*

*The author, who is the director of an institute that is specifically dedicated to scientific research on the survival problem, makes no attempt here to evaluate the evidence for a life after death. He makes no reference, for example, to the famous 'cross correspondence' literature compiled by the S.P.R. in the early part of this century nor to any of the other classic mediumistic cases that have been collected over the years. Instead he plunges direct into a discussion of new ways of approaching the problem and new ways of thinking about it. In particular, he is concerned to question the traditional assumption that: 'the self which survives is the personality we are familiar with from everyday social encounters and our own introspections'. He points to the frequent confusions and contradictions which abound in séance communications as if the communicators were themselves unsure of their own identities! Perhaps, he suggests, we are on the wrong track when we 'equate the survival of consciousness with the survival of personality'.*

* Extracts from Broad, C. D. (1962) *Lectures on Psychical Research* quoted by kind permission of Humanities Press, Inc., New York and Routledge & Kegan Paul, Ltd., London.

*He introduces his hypothetical concept of a 'theta consciousness' defined as that form of consciousness which still persists after the dissolution of the living organism. He then inquires whether any intimations of such a theta consciousness can be discerned in the experiences of those who are still alive. Two special kinds of experience are examined from this point of view. First, the so-called 'out-of-body experience (OBE)' for which there are many accounts. Those who are fortunate enough to have had such experiences claim to know what it is like to be able to see the world, including their own body, from a point somewhere in external space. Now, although this may be thought of as nothing more than a rather special sort of hallucination of high verisimilitude, there is some evidence that veridical information can be acquired paranormally in this condition.*

*Secondly, there are the various mystical experiences which, though they can assume a variety of forms depending on the cultural or religious background of the subject, always seem to involve an absorption of the self into some larger entity. In the ultimate case the individual afterwards describes his state as like being at one with the cosmos as a whole. It is the dissolving of the boundaries of the self that the author calls 'transpersonal consciousness' (TC) and he discusses its connection with mediumship, with the awareness of other peoples' thoughts and emotions that can occur under deep hypnosis and with the effects of psychedelic drugs.*

*However, as the author himself points out, to say that 'consciousness can extend beyond the body is not to say that consciousness is independent of the body, that it can exist apart from the physical organism'. From the standpoint of the survival problem what we really need, both in the case of OBE and of TC, is some evidence that the activities of the central nervous system that are involved in normal perception and cognition are absent or, at any rate, reduced during experiences of this sort. And so far, he admits, no definitive evidence has been forthcoming although recent psychophysiological studies have furnished some small indications that something of this kind may be the case. For example, when an OBE occurs during sleep it does not appear to be accompanied by REMs (rapid eye movements) as ordinary dreaming would be. He might also have mentioned that there is some anecdotal evidence that OBEs can occur while the subject is under anaesthetic or while he is overtly unconscious following an accident and concussion. As regards TCs, he cites evidence to show that there is a global decrease in EEG amplitude during deep hypnosis though he warns that this may reflect no more than a lessening of synchronisation of cortical cell groups. He also mentions the findings of certain Japanese investigators that there is an overall decrease in energy metabolism during Zen meditation. These may be no more than slight clues but the author contends that, at the present time, such research on living subjects opens up the most hopeful avenue for the age-old question of survival.*

*Editor*

## INTRODUCTION

'I should be slightly more annoyed than surprised if I should find myself in some sense persisting immediately after the death of my present body. One can only wait and see, or alternatively (which is no less likely) wait and not see' (Broad, 1962, p. 430). These remarks by C. D. Broad, made at the end of an examination of the survival hypothesis and of some of the evidence for it, tell us two things. The evidence in Broad's opinion was at best suggestive and Broad did not wish to survive.

Most of us would probably agree with Broad's appraisal of the evidence for survival but why did he not want to survive? This may seem a personal matter but it reveals a belief about the possible after-death world which shows how parapsychologists often approach this area of research: 'If there should be another life, one can judge of its possibilities only by analogy with the actualities of life on earth. Nothing that I know of the lives and circumstances of most human beings in the present and in the past encourages me to wish to risk encountering similar possibilities after death' (Broad, 1962, p. x).

The part of this which I want to emphasise is the view that life after death—if there be one—is similar to life before death and that the self which survives is the personality we are familiar with from every day social encounters and our own introspections.*

This kind of reasoning has defined the possibilities and limits of survival research until now. If there can be no survival of consciousness without survival of memories, psychological attitudes, skills and so on, it is obviously useless to explore for a surviving consciousness in their absence. Conversely, if surviving memories, personality traits, etc. are likely to be animated by consciousness then we would obtain evidence for this consciousness if we had evidence for the continuation of the memories, etc.

On the basis of reasoning such as this parapsychologists have focused their attention on memories and other indices of personal

* See Postscript to this chapter.

identity. To illustrate the possibilities and problems of this approach, take the example of a medium who appears to communicate with a deceased person, for instance by describing events from this person's earthly life. The investigator must first satisfy himself that the medium could not have acquired the information normally. If there is evidence that information was obtained by other than known means, i.e. evidence of ESP, another question arises: Did this (ESP) information come from the deceased or did the medium obtain it from some other source?

Most parapsychologists who have worked with mediums have dealt only with the first question—and they have had their hands full. In controlled tests mediums rarely achieve the striking results of many informal 'sittings' or 'readings'. The possibility of chance coincidence therefore becomes of as much concern to the experimenter here as in any other kind of ESP testing. Important contributions to the statistical appraisal of mediumistic statements have been made by H. F. Saltmarsh and S. G. Soal (1930–31), by J. G. Pratt (1948, 1969) and by members of the Psychical Research Foundation (Morris, 1972; Roll and Burdick, 1969; Burdick and Roll, 1971; and Roll, Morris, Damgaard, Klein, and Roll, 1973). In experiments with mediums where these methods were applied it seemed unlikely that the results could be attributed to chance. The same pertains to the reincarnation cases collected by Ian Stevenson (1966). And there are at least a sufficient number of apparitional sightings to consider the ESP hypothesis also for these (Hart, 1956 and Tyrrell, 1961).

There are occasionally reports of physical incidents attributed to the dead, i.e. instances of psychokinesis. A woman recently contacted me because some of the pictures on the walls of her house kept on falling down. She connected the incidents with her deceased husband because the first picture to fall had their marriage licence fastened to its back. Such incidents also convey *information*, i.e. they contain an element of ESP. In the case of the picture, this information is provided by the selection of an object associated with the deceased from other objects which might have been affected by PK.

At the same time as we only take seriously ostensible cases of survival which include evidence for ESP, this same evidence becomes the source of the major counterhypothesis to survival. It is easy to see why this is so. The moment we have verified the earthly circumstances or psychological characteristics of a deceased person who seems to communicate through a medium, we have found an existing source from which the medium might have obtained this information by ESP without relying on the supposed communicator. The same applies to other apparent manifestations of the dead.

The theory that apparent communications can be explained by the medium's ESP powers has been reinforced by some peculiarities in this type of material. There is a great deal of confusion about the 'ownership' of memories. Sometimes a communicator has a clear memory of an event which never took place or he may 'remember' something which happened in the life of another communicator. There are occasionally communications from persons who later turn out to be alive. Other times entirely fictitious communicators appear; these are not only accepted by the medium as genuine but also by the other communicators. Sometimes a communicator who first announces himself as one person, later turns out to be somebody else.

If the personality which survives death is essentially the personality which existed before death, we might expect lapses of memory. It is more difficult to explain confusion about the very 'ownership' of memories and about personal identity. As a rule material such as this is rejected as evidence for survival. Instead it is generally supposed that the mixed-up memories and the fictitious communicators are the results of unconscious processes in the medium. It is then a short step to say that this is also true for the verified communicators and that they too are fictitious characters built around a core of ESP information which the medium has obtained from existing sources. A great deal more has been said for and against the evidence that the cluster of memories, psychological traits, etc. which together we refer to as human personality survives the death of the body. But there is a question to which we have not seriously addressed ourselves. This is the question whether we can equate the survival of consciousness with the survival of personality.

It is part of what we mean by survival that the consciousness which may survive death was present before death. As Broad suggested, it should therefore be possible to get an idea of what life *after* death may be like by examining life *before* death. But to say that post mortem consciousness already exists in the living is not the same as saying that this is the consciousness of everyday waking experience, i.e. the consciousness which is associated with the dispositions, memories, skills and so on which together make up what we refer to as the personality of a living being.

## SURVIVAL RESEARCH WITH THE LIVING

To facilitate the discussion, I shall refer to the consciousness which may survive death as theta consciousness (theta is taken from the first letter of thanatos, the Greek word for death, not from the brain wave of that name). There are several different kinds of consciousness of which the waking consciousness most of us experience most of the time is only one. In addition to dream consciousness, of which several types exist, there are states of consciousness which result from being hypnotised, engaging in meditation, taking drugs and so on. The question at issue is what the characteristics of theta consciousness may be.

First, theta consciousness must be capable of existing without the living organism. Secondly, if there is interaction between the deceased after death—and perhaps between the dead and the living, as in mediumistic communications—then theta consciousness must possess psychical abilities (or perhaps itself be a 'state' of psychical awareness or activity).

The state of consciousness we are looking for then is one in which awareness is not limited by the boundaries of the body and in which it becomes possible to apprehend events beyond the range of sense perception at those locations to which consciousness is 'extended'.

From time to time people have reported that their self or 'I' seemed to move beyond the boundaries of the body. The experience ranges from the feeling that something akin to waking consciousness leaves the physical body and occupies another distinct location in space and time to the global feeling that the self simultaneously occupies all space and time. The first kind of experience is found in so-called out-of-body experiences (OBEs), also referred to as 'travelling clairvoyance', 'ESP projection', etc. The second kind goes under an even greater variety of names depending upon the cultural and religious background of the person. Zen Buddhists refer to it as 'satori' (enlightenment) and Hindus call it 'satchi-dananda' (existence-knowledge-bliss). It has been called the 'peak experience' by Abraham Maslow (1964). Here I shall use the phrase 'transpersonal consciousness' (TC) where transpersonal is defined (by Webster) as 'extending beyond the personal or individual'.

## OUT-OF-BODY EXPERIENCES

A forty-seven year old woman recently told me about the following experience in a letter. 'All my life I have been able to leave my body while asleep . . . The most unusual experience . . . occurred in August 1971. I knew that I was asleep and it was time to get up and that I must return to the body to wake it up. I came through the air, hovered just under the ceiling, went through my kitchen and hall and into the bedroom where I saw my own body sleeping on the stomach in a familiar position, face turned to the west. What a shock to look down on one's self and see one's own face and hair. I quickly came down and entered the body from the back. It is even a greater shock to make contact with one's own body. It takes a few seconds for the flying body to fit into the same position as the sleeping body, then the intelligence tells the body to move its hands and open its eyes. I woke myself up and found myself in the same position I had seen from the air.'

Out-of-body experiences may convince the person that his consciousness can exist apart from the body but how is this belief to be tested? At the present we can only distinguish such experiences from private dreams and phantasies if they are associated with ESP or PK phenomena, that is, if there is evidence that the person is able actually to observe events at the location to which his consciousness had moved or evidence that he can interact with physical objects there. It is seldom, however, that people can induce OBEs on demand. As a result only few experimental studies have been done in this area until recently. One of these was an exploratory test by Charles T. Tart (1969) with a young woman who sometimes had the sensation at night of floating near the ceiling of her bedroom and looking down at her body. Tart suggested that she write the numbers one to ten on ten slips of paper and pick one at random every night without looking at it and then place it on her bedroom table out of sight from the bed but visible from the ceiling. When the woman reported having done this seven times, succeeding each time, Tart invited her to try the same in a psychophysiology laboratory. For each of the four nights she slept there, Tart wrote a five digit number, taken from a random number table, and placed it on a shelf seven feet above her bed. The young woman several times reported out-of-body experiences but only during the last night she thought she saw the number and correctly gave this as 25132. Although only one guess was made this result is statistically highly significant. Tart was not observing her all the time so fraud was not definitely ruled out. She was, however, wired to an electroencephalograph which recorded her brain waves so she could not surreptitiously have left the bed without disrupting the recording.

Another OBE subject studied by Tart gave less definite ESP evidence. Tart took brain wave recordings in both studies but found no consistent pattern.

OBE research is now conducted both at the American Society for Psychical Research in New York and at the Psychical Research Foundation in Durham, North Carolina. No definite results have yet been reported but it may be of interest to outline the procedures used. In both places, attempts are made to determine whether the self in any sense 'leaves' the physical body as against the possibility that ESP impressions are transmitted to the body and that the travelling aspect is only imaginary. At the American Society Dr Karlis Osis is using a specially designed target box to help clarify this question. One of the targets sometimes used in this box is the small letter 'd'. The box is enclosed except at one end where there is an opening. A mirror arrangement causes the 'd' to appear as a 'b' from the opening. The subject, who is in another room, is instructed to 'go' to the target room in his out-of-body form and to report the target. The assumption is that if the subject uses ordinary ESP, the box covering is no impediment and he will 'see' the letter 'd'. If, however, he is having an out-of-body experience, the target box will appear opaque. In that case he will only be able to 'see' the letter from the open end—and report a 'b.'

During the experiments, brain wave recordings are taken from the subject and compared with the recordings before and after the OBE. At the Psychical Research Foundation we also take brain wave recordings from OBE subjects. At the present time we use more or less standard ESP targets. Our main emphasis is the detection of the OBE subject at the target location. There are anecdotal reports that a person who has left his body was seen or felt at the location to which he has moved and, occasionally, that he physically affected an object in that location, say removed a book from its shelf. At the present we are mainly using persons as detectors but we are beginning to explore animals and physical instruments for this purpose also.

The possible relevance of out-of-body experiences to survival has been noted by many parapsychologists. The topic was of especial interest to the late Hornell Hart. He made a survey (1956) of reported apparitions of the dead and compared these with apparitions of living persons when they were having out-of-body experiences. Hart concluded that 'the projected personality carries full memories and purposes'. Because conscious OBE apparitions of living persons are in many respects similar to apparitions of the dead, Hart thought that the latter also 'carry with them the memories and purposes of the personalities which they represent, and thus constitute evidence of survival of personality beyond bodily death'.

Few parapsychologists are ready to accept the survival hypothesis on the basis of apparitional sightings. The cases are too scarce and uncertain to accept as proof of anything. But Hart's reasoning that we may learn something about a possible life after death by studies of out-of-body experiences in the living seems sound. The finding which, in my opinion, would tip the scales in favour of survival would be evidence that the activities of the central nervous system involved in perceptual and other conscious activities are reduced during out-of-body experiences. So far there are no indications that this is the case. It does appear, however that rapid eye movements (REMs), from which one can tell whether or not a person is having visual dreams, are absent or reduced during out-of-body experiences. If this should be substantiated, OBEs may at least represent a different kind of mental activity than ordinary dreaming.

Whether or not the consciousness which seems to leave the body temporarily during an out-of-body experience is the same consciousness which may leave it permanently after death, OBE consciousness is similar to the kind which we usually have in mind when we think of survival after death. But this is not the only possibility. For the remainder of this paper I shall examine the possibility that the 'expanded' type of consciousness I referred to as transpersonal consciousness may survive death. This possibility has been neglected by parapsychologists and I think it may be useful to bring it into the picture together with the other states of consciousness which may survive death.

## TRANSPERSONAL CONSCIOUSNESS

After six years of Zen meditation a Canadian housewife had an 'enlightenment' experience where the world became 'a vast "geometry of existence" of unspeakable profundity, . . . (a) multidimensional . . . complex of dynamic force, to contact which one must abandon one's normal level of consciousness.' At the same time as 'The physical world is an infinity of movement, of Time-Existence, . . . it is an infinity of Silence and Voidness. Each object is thus transparent. Everything has its own special inner character, its own . . . "life in time," but at the same time there is no place where there is emptiness, where one object does not flow into another.' She felt 'a consciousness which is neither myself nor not myself . . . It is like a stream into which I have flowed and, joyously, is carrying me beyond myself' (Kapleau, 1965). This experience did not cause her to reject the familiar world as unreal but it made her see the latter as less 'complete' and also less 'important' than the world which was revealed to her.

How does the subjective TC view of reality compare with the world of science and ordinary experience? TC experiences show interesting similarities to descriptions of the world by modern physicists. The idea that ordinary sensory perception only reveals part of the physical world is reminiscent of statements such as the one by James Jeans (1947) that the material world is only a 'cross-section of the world of reality.' Other aspects of the TC experiences of the Canadian housewife match A. S. Eddington's (1931) assertion that '. . . the stuff of the world is mind stuff' and Werner Heisenberg's description of reality as '. . . a complicated tissue of events', (1958) in which 'it is not the geometric forms, but the dynamic laws concerning movement . . . which are permanent' (1966). Lawrence LeShan (1966) has drawn attention to these and other similarities between the world as experienced by 'mystics' and as described by physicists.

If the real physical world is directly apprehended during TC experiences, we might expect the person at times to become aware of ordinary events in addition to the 'complex of dynamic force' of the physical world. Such awareness might appear as instances of what we call ESP.

It is interesting that ESP abilities are often said to develop in meditators and others who seek TC experiences. It is usually not their purpose to develop such abilities. If ESP incidents are treated seriously, as a rule it is because they are seen as objective indications that the meditator has attained or is in the process of attaining a TC state. A story from the life of the late Chinese Zen (Ch'an) teacher, Hsu Yun, illustrates. After many years of meditation 'the master succeeded in realizing singleness of mind, and in his fifty-sixth year, one evening, in Kao Ming monastery at Yangchow, after a long meditation, he opened his eyes and saw everything inside and outside the monastery. Through the wall, he saw a monk urinating outside, a guest monk in the latrine and far away, boats plying . . . the river and trees on both its banks' (Yu, 1969).

TC experiences are also reported by mediums and others

apparently endowed with unusual psychical abilities. The medium, Mrs Coombe Tennant (known as 'Mrs Willett') once said after a mediumistic sitting; 'The room seemed full of unseen presences and of their blessing; it was as if barriers were swept away and I and they became one. I had no sense of personality in the unseen element—it was just there and utterly satisfying' (Balfour, 1935).

To Rosalind Heywood (1964), a member of the Council of the Society for Psychical Research who has described apparent ESP experiences in her books, '. . . it seems as if one consciousness pervades the whole of Nature and finds expression, not only through the visible trees and flowers and birds and animals, but also through myriads of invisible entities which form an inner part of the composite life of the wild.'

The unitary experience of TC is sometimes preceded by the feeling of losing one's personal identity. The Canadian housewife mentioned before had a traumatic experience prior to her feeling of oneness with the world: '. . . secret resentments and hidden fears . . . flowed out of me like poisons. Tears gushed out and so weakened me I had to lie down. Yet a deep happiness was there . . . Slowly my focus changed: "I'm dead! There's nothing to call *me*! There never was a *me*! It's an allegory, a mental image, a pattern upon which nothing was ever modeled." I grew dizzy with delight. Solid objects appeared as shadows, and everything my eyes fell upon was radiantly beautiful' (Kapleau, 1965).

Mrs Coombe Tennant once said as she was coming out of an apparent trance communication with the deceased Frederick Myers: 'Oh! . . . Fred. So strange to be somebody else. To feel somebody's heart beating inside you, and somebody else's mind inside your mind!' (Balfour, 1935). Mrs Eileen Garrett (1943), another widely investigated medium, said that when she practiced her mediumship, 'I have an inner feeling of participating, in a very unified way, with what I observe—by which I mean that I have no sense of I or any other, but a close association with, an immersion in, the phenomena.'

## Experimental and Clinical Studies

Psychologists and psychiatrists are becoming interested in the nature of transpersonal consciousness and a few exploratory studies have been conducted which are relevant to our understanding of the nature of the TC experience and of the extent to which this experience is associated with psi phenomena. In addition to meditators and mediums, subjects in deep hypnosis or under the influence of drugs have reported TC experiences.

In the attempts to understand hypnosis 'in its clearest and strongest form' Spencer Sherman (1971) decided to investigate it 'as it exists when unclouded by suggestions, and when the subject is deepest in it.'

He found three types of experiences to be characteristic of the most profound depths reported by his subjects. These were 'Being everything . . . feeling oneness with everything' and 'blankness; absolute mental quiet: no thoughts, images, etc.; voidness; nothing happening; and loss of knowledge of your individual identity; no self or ego.' Sherman reported a few ESP experiences among his subjects during deep hypnosis but he did not give details.

In a study by Charles Tart (1969) involving 'mutual hypnosis' he instructed two subjects to give each other suggestions and hereby achieved a very deep trance in both. The change in consciousness which most impressed the subjects 'was the feeling of *merging* with each other at times, especially in the final mutual hypnosis session. This seemed like a partial fusion of identities, a partial loss of the distinction between I and Thou.' During the last session Tart suggested the two hypnotised subjects each have a dream. The dreams began differently, but each dream ended with the subjects climbing upward on a swaying support, a rope ladder in one case and a golden rope in the other. Tart then asked the subjects to 'go exploring' together and describe their experiences aloud. The subjects found themselves together in a hallucinatory world which they described as a kind of 'heaven.' Some of the details of the experiences which came out afterwards raised the possibility that the subjects had been communicating by tele-pathy or that they had actually been together 'in' another world.

Stanislav Grof (1972)* heads a research project in which LSD is administered to terminal cancer patients to study the effect of the drug in alleviating fear of death. Grof reports that LSD sometimes results in an 'experience of cosmic unity.' He writes, 'The basic characteristics of this experience are transcendence of the subject–object dichtomy, exceptionally strong positive affect (peace, tranquility, serenity, bliss), a special feeling of sacredness, transcendence of time and space, experience of pure being ('eter-

---

* Extracts from Stanislav Grof (1972) are the copyright of the *Journal of Trans-personal Psychology*, **4** no. 1. Reprinted by permission of the Transpersonal Institute, 2637 Marshall Drive, Palo Alto, Ca. 94303.

nity now and infinity here'), and a richness of insights of cosmic relevance.' Changes of personal identity are also reported. Sometimes 'The subject experiences complete identification with another person and loses to a great degree the awareness of his own original identity. This identification is total and complex; it involves the body image, the full range of emotions and psychological attitudes, facial expression, gestures and mannerisms, postures, movements, and even the inflection of voice . . . the subject can experience identification with his close relatives, friends, acquaintances, teachers, political figures, etc.'

At times there are ESP incidents. These are as a rule more apparent than real but 'Occasionally the LSD subject can be unusually accurate in his awareness of the sitter's ideation and emotions without even looking at him. Two subjects who have the session at the same time can share many ideas or have parallel experiences without much verbal communication and interchange. Exceptionally, a claim made by an LSD subject about telepathic contact with a distant person can be supported by objective evidence obtained by independent investigation' (Grof, 1972).

## Parapsychological Studies

In the early days of the Society for Psychical Research, it was thought that ESP and hypnosis were closely related. In fact, some of the first systematic studies of hypnosis were done by members of this Society. But there were only a few ESP tests in which there were adequate precautions against sensory cues. Among these were the experiments in which the hypnotist induced a trance at distances ranging from about one third to two thirds of a mile from the subject (Myers 1886–87, 129 ff; Gurney 1888–89, 221 ff).

From the present point of view the early experiments in 'community of sensation' are especially interesting though experimentally weak since the hypnotist and the subject were in the same room. Some of these tests are mentioned by J. Fraser Nicol (1968). In the experiments, reported by Edmund Gurney in 1883, the subject apparently could taste substances which the hypnotist had in his mouth. For instance, when the hypnotist took some bitter aloes, the subject felt 'as if I'd been eating acid drops'. In another experiment Gurney decided on a spontaneous test and suddenly pinched the arm of the hypnotist. The entranced subject, who was sitting some eight feet away with her back toward them, 'instantly started up, as if in great excitement, rubbed the *exactly* corresponding place on her own person, and complained of violent pain'.

In a review of the more recent and better conducted experiments involving hypnosis, Charles Honorton and Stanley Krippner (1969) concluded that there was an overall tendency for results in ESP to improve under hypnosis. They attributed this, not to the specific suggestions given the subjects, but to relaxation and to reductions of 'reality testing' and 'attentive activity'.

Meditation is one of the oldest and most widely used methods to develop TC. In most forms of TC meditation, the person first tries to enter a deep state of tranquility, yet remains fully awake (Wallace and Benson, 1972). Usually, the mind is either kept blank or is engaged in some simple task, such as repeating a word mentally or visualising an object, with the hope that this will reduce discursive thinking and allow the meditator to experience the unity between himself and the rest of the world. Sometimes rhythmic chanting or movements are used instead of silent meditation. It is interesting that mediums and psychics sometimes use comparable procedures to evoke ESP impressions.

One of the psychics studied by W. H. C. Tenhaeff 'often started tapping his feet more or less rhythmically. This apparently caused a state of relaxation, which facilitated "rising" of telepathic impressions. [He] . . . also used to blindfold himself when the impression did not come easily to him. "I have to shut myself off [from] the outside world for a moment," he would say. Thus, blindfolded he then started tapping his feet.'

In a survey of highly successful ESP subjects, Rhea White (1964) found that they would first try to enter a state of relaxation as a preparation for the task. At the same time, they remained alert and cleared their minds of extraneous thoughts either by keeping their minds blank or focusing their attention on some one thing, such as a mental image. After a period of waiting, this image would be released and an ESP impression would enter consciousness.

In an exploratory ESP study with a group of meditators at the American Society for Psychical Research, Karlis Osis and Edwin Bokert (1971) concluded that the people who did best in ESP had a 'feeling of merging with the others . . . and a feeling of oneness as if the boundaries between "what is me and what is not me" were dissolving.' At the Foundation for Research on the Nature of Man, Francine Matas and Lee Pantas (1971) in a pilot test found that PK subjects who had practiced meditation or similar forms of self-development were more successful than the control group.

And in a brief session with students at the City University of New York, Gertrude Schmeidler (1970) found a significant increase in ESP scoring after Swami Madhavananda Saraswati had given a short instruction on meditation and breathing.

## Psychophysiological Studies

There is a question about transpersonal consciousness which is crucial to the survival question and which we have not yet considered. If TC experiences are associated with (or perhaps identical with) ESP awareness, this suggests that the boundaries of the body are not the boundaries of the mind. To say that consciousness can extend *beyond* the body, however, is not to say that consciousness is *independent* of the body, that it can exist apart from the physical organism. TC experience and ESP awareness may both be functions of the central nervous system. Is there any way to determine whether or not TC can exist apart from that system?

So far, the best objective indicators of states of consciousness are brain waves. A brain wave, as any other electric wave, shows two things, frequency and amplitude.

Most brain wave studies have been concerned with frequency. Studies of meditators (Wallace *et al.*, 1972) suggest that the alpha wave (and sometimes theta) may be associated with TC. A brain showing alpha has been compared to an idling motor. In other words the brain seems to be in a state of readiness in which there is a lessening of cortical activities.

T. Hirai found a decrease of respiratory rate and slowing of EEG pattern during Zen meditation. Y. Sugi *et al.* also found reductions of respiratory rate, as well as of tidal volume and $O_2$ consumption during Zen meditation, indicating a decrease of energy metabolism to lower than basic metabolism. Sugi suggests this may be the result of a decrease of energy metabolism in the brain. (Kasamatsu and Hirai, 1969).

With respect to amplitude, Sherman (1971) found that 'very deep hypnosis is often characterized by a continuous global decrease in EEG amplitude, and that it is almost always characterized by briefer periods of global EEG amplitude diminution to very low levels.' (As other investigators, Sherman found no EEG differences between the waking state and what is usually considered deep hypnosis.) He equates this with 'less brain electrical activity . . . It is possible that this phenomenon indicates that subjects have ceased all normal activity; the minimal electrical activity that remains may reflect undifferentiated awareness, or events from deeper or lower nervous system loci which have no conscious reflection.' This appears to be the kind of evidence we are looking for. Unfortunately, Sherman's interpretation is open to question since a decrease in EEG amplitude may only reflect a lessening of synchronisation of cortical cell groups.

A different finding has been observed in Zen meditation. Kasamatsu and Hirai report that in the progress of Zen meditation, alpha waves increase in amplitude and decrease in frequency (sometimes theta appears in the latter stage of meditation) (Kasamatsu et al., 1969). Zen, however, is an active and intense form of meditation which may involve a restructuring of the perceptual world rather than a withdrawal from it. At the present time we do not know the real meaning of amplitude changes. Conceivably, different types of meditation may result in different EEG amplitudes.

Another promising topic for research into the psychophysiology of TC is the exploration of differences between the two brain hemispheres. There is considerable evidence that the two hemispheres of the cortex are differentially involved in many aspects of information processing. Specifically the left hemisphere is (for right handed people) apparently more involved with language and linear, or sequential, information processing; the right hemisphere is apparently more involved in global, spatial, simultaneous information processing such as synchronised motor activity (Sperry, 1968; Ornstein, 1972; Kinsbourne, 1972). Desynchronisation or blockage of the alpha rhythm is considered evidence of hemispheric activation; thus asymmetrical deactivation would indicate the relative involvement of the two hemispheres. Out-of-body experiences and transpersonal consciousness may both represent externalisation of the self from the body, with the former involving primarily left hemisphere (linear, sequential information processing) and the latter involving primarily right hemisphere (global, nonsequential) information processing. Such a possibility could be assessed in part from comparison of left and right hemisphere occipital EEG records in persons having OBE and TC experiences.

The discovery of an apparent relationship between alpha waves,

TC and ESP makes alpha biofeedback a possible means for developing TC and ESP. A beginning has been made by Charles Honorton (1971) and others to explore biofeedback as a way to develop ESP.

## CONCLUSION

Broad's suggestion that we may survive as a more or less well defined, 'field'* fits in well with possibilities we have examined. Broad limited this field by assuming that consciousness is the result of interactions between a personality and its environment. But consciousness, it seems, can exist without any of the (other) components of personality. Indeed descriptions of transpersonal consciousness suggest that the more 'detached' awareness is from the perceptions, memories and emotions of personal existence, the richer and more vivid this awareness becomes.

In out-of-body experiences the 'field of consciousness' is usually limited to the familiar personality existing in a given location in space and time. In transpersonal states, consciousness sometimes seems to encompass all there is. These two forms of consciousness may be the extremes in a wide spectrum of possible states before and after bodily death.

If transpersonal consciousness represents the after-death state at least for some people at some times, this might help us understand some of the peculiarities in the survival data. If the memories, dispositions and skills of the deceased do not necessarily 'belong' to the consciousness associated with them in life but can be activated by others, the confusions of memories and personal identity so common in mediumistic studies is easier to understand.

It has not been my purpose to evaluate the strength of the evidence for a life after death. Hopefully psychophysiological and other studies of persons during OBE and TC experiences should help to determine whether or not there can be experience independently of the central nervous system.

Paradoxically, we may obtain better evidence for or against survival through studies of living subjects than of ostensible deceased communicators. More importantly, living subjects provide easier access to the characteristics of the consciousness which may survive and of the space in which it survives. This should result in a more effective model of postmortem survival with which to explore new data and interpret the old.

*See Postscript to this chapter

## A POSTSCRIPT ON BROAD'S THEORY OF SURVIVAL

Broad says: 'It seems to me that a *necessary*, though by no means sufficient, condition for survival is that the whole or some considerable part of the *dispositional basis* of a human being's personality should persist, and retain at least the main outline of its characteristic type of organization, for some time after the disintegration of his brain and nervous system' (author's italics, Broad (1962), 414).

It was this surviving dispositional basis of personality that Broad called the '$\psi$-component' and suggested that such a $\psi$-component could be thought of as analogous to a persistent vortex in the old fashioned ether carrying modulations imposed on it by experiences had by the person with whose physical body it was formerly associated as a kind of 'field'. He considered that the concept of survival presupposed that the self would occupy some kind of body in the next life: 'speaking for myself' he declares (*idem*, 414), 'I find it more and more difficult, the more I try and go into concrete detail, to conceive of a person so unlike the only ones I know anything about, and from whom my whole notion of personality is necessarily derived, as an unembodied person would inevitably be'. If, however, we do suppose that: 'a discarnate $\psi$-component is *wholly unembodied*, then much the most likely alternative (excluding for the present purpose complete extinction) would be mere persistence without any kind of associated experiences. For we know that, when sensory stimuli acting on a man's body from without are reduced to a minimum, he tends to fall asleep. And we know that, when in addition sensory stimuli from within his body are reduced to a minimum, his sleep tends to be dreamless' (author's italics, *idem*, 422).

Thus Broad's view that consciousness can only result from stimulation led him to the opinion that unembodied survival would probably be unconscious. But the material reviewed in this chapter suggests, on the contrary, that a reduction of external and internal stimuli may lead to increased states of awareness including transpersonal consciousness and that in such states the subject may reach higher levels of consciousness than when he experiences himself and the world in terms of his individual personality.

## REFERENCES

Balfour, Gerald William. (1935) 'A study of the psychological aspects of Mrs Willett's mediumship, and of the statements of the communicators concerning process.' *Proc. S.P.R.*, **43**, 43–318

Broad, C. D. (1962) *Lectures on Psychical Research*. Routledge, London; Humanities Press, New York

Burdick, D. S., and Roll, W. G. (1971) 'Differential weighting of ESP responses.' *J. Amer. S.P.R.*, **65**, 173–184

Eddington, A. S. (1931) *The Nature of the Physical World*. Macmillan, New York

Garrett, Eileen. (1943) *Awareness*, p. 113, Creative Age Press, Inc., New York

Grof, Stanislav. (1972) 'Varieties of transpersonal experiences: Observations from LSD psychotherapy.' *J. Transpersonal Psychol.*, **4**, 45–80

Gurney, Edmund. (1888–89) 'Hypnotism and telepathy.' *Proc. S.P.R.*, **5**, 216–259

Hart, Hornell and Associated Collaborators. (1956) 'Six theories about apparitions.' *Pro. S.P.R.*, **50**, 153–239

Heisenberg, Werner. (1958) *Physics and Philosophy*. Harper, New York

Heisenberg, Werner. (1966) *Philosophic Problems of Nuclear Science*. Faucett, Greenwich, Connecticut

Heywood, Rosalind. (1964) *The Infinite Hive*. Chatto and Windus, Ltd., London

Honorton, C., Davidson, R., and Bindler, P. (1971) 'Feedback-augmented EEG alpha, shifts in subjective state, and ESP card-guessing performance.' *J. Amer. S.P.R.*, **65**, 308–323

Honorton, C., and Krippner, S. (1969) 'Hypnosis and ESP performance: a review of the literature' *J. Amer. S.P.R.*, **63**, 214–252

Jeans, James. (1947) 'Some problems of philosophy.' In S. Cummings & R. Linscott (Eds.), *Man and the Universe: The Philosophers of Science*. Random, New York

Kapleau, Philip. (1965) *The Three Pillars of Zen*, pp. 267–268. Beacon Press, Boston

Kasamatsu, Akira and Hirai, Tomio. (1969) 'An electroencephalographic study on the Zen meditation (Zazen).' In Charles T. Tart (Ed.) *Altered States of Consciousness*. John Wiley & Sons, New York

Kinsbourne, Marcel. (1972) 'Eye-head turning indicates cerebral laterialization.' *Science*, **176**, 539–541

LeShan, Lawrence. (1969) 'Physicists and mystics: Similarities in world view.' *J. Transpersonal Psychol.*, **1**, 1–20

Maslow, Abraham. (1964) *Religions, Values and Peak Experiences.* Ohio State University Press, Columbus, Ohio

Matas, Francine and Pantas, Lee. (1971) 'A PK experiment comparing meditating versus non-meditating subjects.' *Proc. Parapsychol. Assn.*, **8**, 12–13

Morris, Robert Lyle. (1972) 'An exact method for evaluating preferentially matched free-response material.' *J. Amer. S.P.R.*, **66**, 401–407

Myers, F. W. H. (1886–87) 'On telepathic hypnotism, and its relation to other forms of hypnotic suggestion.' *Proc. S.P.R.*, **4**, 127–188

Nicol, J. Fraser. 'Classic Experiments of Telepathy under Hypnosis' in Cavanna, Roberto, and Montague Ullman (Eds.) (1967) *Proceedings of an International Conference on Hypnosis, Drugs, Dreams, and Psi.* Parapsychology Foundation, 1968, New York

Ornstein, Robert E. (1972) *The Psychology of Consciousness.* W. H. Freeman, San Francisco

Osis, Karlis, and Bokert, Edwin. (1971) 'ESP and changed states of consciousness induced by meditation.' *J. Amer. S.P.R.*, **65**, 17–65

Pratt, J. G., and Birge, W. R. (1948) 'Appraising verbal test material in parapsychology.' *J. Parapsychol.*, **12**, 236–256

Pratt, J. G. (1969) 'On the evaluation of verbal material in parapsychology.' *Parapsychological Monographs, No. 10*, New York: Parapsychology Foundation

Roll, W. G., and Burdick, D. S. (1969) 'Statistical models for the assessment of verbal and other ESP responses.' *J. Amer. S.P.R.*, **63**, 287–302

Roll, W. G., Morris, R. L., Damgaard, J. A., Klein, J. and Roll. M. (1973) 'Free verbal response experiments with Lalsingh Harribance.' *J. Amer. S.P.R.*, **67**, 197–207

Saltmarsh, H. F., and Soal, S. G. (1930–31) 'A method of estimating the supernormal content of mediumistic communications.' *Proc. S.P.R.*, **39**, 266–271

Schmeidler, Gertrude R. (1970) 'High ESP scores after a Swami's brief instruction in meditation and breathing.' *J. Amer. S.P.R.*, **64**, 100–103

Sherman, Spencer Elliott. (1971) *Very Deep Hypnosis: An Experimental and Electroencephalographic Investigation.* Stanford University. Doctoral Dissertation

Sperry, R. W. (1968) 'Hemisphere deconnection and unity in conscious awareness.' *Amer. Psychologist*, **23**, 723–733

Stevenson, Ian. (1966) 'Twenty Cases Suggestive of Reincarnation.' *Proc. Amer. S.P.R.*, **26**, (monograph)

Tart, Charles T. (Ed.) (1969) *Altered States of Consciousness: A Book of Readings.* John Wiley & Sons, New York

Tenhaeff, W. H. C. (1966) 'Some aspects of parapsychological research in the Netherlands.' *Int. J. Neuropsychiatry,* **2,** 408–419

Tyrrell, G. N. M. (1961) *Apparitions.* University Books, Inc., New York

Wallace, Robert Keith and Benson, Herbert. (1972) 'The physiology of meditation.' *Scientific American,* **226,** 84–91

White, Rhea A. (1964) 'A comparison of old and new methods of response to targets in ESP experiments.' *J. Amer. S.P.R.,* **58,** 21–56

Yu, Lu K'uan. (1969) *The Secrets of Chinese Meditation.* Rider, London

# POSTSCRIPT
Arthur Koestler

A postscript to a symposium is usually intended to provide the reader with a summary or overall view of the varied and sometimes disjointed contributions—to trace the pattern in the mosaic. In the present case such an undertaking would be redundant, because the editor himself has provided concise summaries preceding each chapter; and if the reader, after finishing the book, will peruse these seven synopses consecutively, he will obtain a gratifying birds-eye view of its rich contents. Thus instead of another summing up, I shall confine myself to a few subjective comments.

The title, *New Directions in Parapsychology,* sounds matter-of-fact, yet it seems to imply that all was not well with the old directions: that they were leading into a cul-de-sac. Most veterans of this field of research will probably agree that this was indeed the case. One of the reasons for it has been underlined in Charles Honorton's paper: 'Until recently . . . little systematic research has been directed towards the elucidation of subjective states associated with paranormal functioning. In view of the behaviouristic *Zeitgeist,* it is perhaps not surprising that early proponents of the card-guessing paradigm . . . largely disregarded their subjects' internal states . . .'

One might say that parapsychology was more concerned with the para than with psychology. Given the circumstances, this was almost unavoidable. As John Beloff commented: 'The Rhine school of parapsychology thought to beat behaviourism at its own game by showing that anti-behaviourist conclusions could be arrived at on the basis of impeccably objectivist data'. To have obtained these data with dogged perseverance, undeterred by academic hostility and ignorant derision, is the Rhine school's historic achievement. It was only made possible by the self-imposed limitations which Honorton mentions. One of the cornerstones of scientific methodology is the formula *ceteris paribus*— 'other things being equal'. But other things are never equal where human subjects are concerned. Not even their reactions to the gross chemical impact of drugs are equal. Clinical studies have

shown that about one-third of the American hospital population
are placebo-reactors (Cole, 1961). Given the appropriate suggestion, they will react to barbiturates as if they were amphetamines,
to amphetamines as if they were barbiturates, and to
placebos as if they were one or the other, as the case may be.
Their states of consciousness interact with, and often override,
the effect of the chemical input. It seems obvious that the effect of
a psi input—whatever it consists of—is even more dependent on
the 'hidden variables' of the subject's general character-disposi-
tion and particular state of mind at the time of the experimental
test or spontaneous occurrence.

Thus one may wonder whether the parapsychologist's quest for
the ideal experiment—repeatable at will, yielding predictable
results—will not turn out to be a wild-goose chase. In spite of his
customary caution, John Beloff in his Introduction expresses the
hope that parapsychology is 'edging its way towards a solution of
the problem of repeatability'. He may be right, but I do not feel so
sure about it. A parabola edges its way towards its asymptotes
without ever achieving union. The nearest we have come to a
repeatable experiment is in the field of automated animal experimentation, described by John Randall in Chapter 4. Perhaps with
mice, gerbils and chicks the 'other things' are more equal, and
interfere less with the functioning of the psi faculty. But ask any
writer, or painter, or scientist to define the precise conditions under
which the creative spark will repeatably and predictably ignite the
vapours in his mind! And creativity is a less elusive and mysterious
faculty than psi.

The above is by no means intended to belittle the parapsychologist's patient efforts to elucidate the personality structures and
states of consciousness which enhance the psi faculty, and the
experimental conditions best suited to trigger it off. On the contrary, I consider these efforts—described in the chapters by Honorton and Rao—as perhaps the most significant among the 'new
directions' in parapsychology. I still remember with what enthusiasm I read about Gertrude Schmeidler's pioneer work some
twenty years ago; 'sheep' and 'goats' appeared as a first step
towards a taxonomy of potential psi subjects. In more than a
quarter-million card trials with more than 1100 subjects the
sheep scored significantly and persistently higher than the goats.
It looked so beautifully simple, almost self-evident: have we not
always been taught that faith can move mountains—i.e., perform
feats of PK? Unfortunately things turned out not to be as simple as
that. Beloff and others found that in some studies the goats,

perhaps out of sheer perversity, did better than the sheep; and a careful study of Rao's paper reveals that the singling out of any other personality factor led to similarly contradictory or inconclusive results. The combination of several factors, as attempted by Rao and Kanthamani, seems a more holistic and promising approach. Yet ironically, Rao's composite portrait of the potentially high scoring ESP subject (p. 68) is in almost every respect the exact opposite of Pratt's description (p. 117) of the highest scoring person known at present—Pavel Stepanek. The situation reminds one of a remark by the science-fiction writer Poul Anderson: 'I have yet to see any problem, however complicated, which, when you looked at it in the right way, did not become still more complicated'.

But that need not unduly worry the parapsychologist; other sciences have found themselves in similar predicaments in the past or present. The subatomic world composed of electrons and protons looked complicated enough, but when the physicists looked at it in the right way, it became still more complicated, with a hundred elementary particles instead of two. The physicist's trouble is that the subatomic phenomena which he manipulates can no longer be fitted into the spatio-temporal framework of naive realism and conventional physics. The parapsychologist's trouble is equally fundamental. He too can manipulate, up to a point, the manifestations of psi in his laboratory, but he is unable to fit them into the framework of conventional psychology, and knows next to nothing of their physiological correlates, evolutionary origin and biological value—what psi is 'for' in the general scheme of things. We do not even know whether, in evolutionary terms, psi is an *emergent* faculty—somehow related to man's spirituality— which gradually unfolds, like sentience and consciousness, with each upward step on the evolutionary ladder, or whether on the contrary extra-sensory perception is an archaic and primitive form of communication which has been superseded by more efficient forms of sensory perception (but in this case, what about PK?). Needless to say, the question is of fundamental importance, not only to the parapsychologist, but also to the philosopher and metaphysician. This alone would make the pursuit of parapsychology an immensely worthwhile undertaking; and several chapters in the present volume indicate that, even if the researchers of the younger generation have not come up with final answers, they are learning to ask the pertinent questions.

One such question is briefly, perhaps all too briefly, discussed in Helmut Schmidt's paper: the apparently non-causal nature of subatomic physics on the one hand, and of parapsychological phenomena on the other. 'It was', Schmidt remarks, 'one of the boldest steps of modern physics to take the possibility of pure chance (as opposed to the strict causality of classical physics) as a basic element in nature seriously.' If the physicist is not afraid to postulate a non-causal substratum on which the world of everyday phenomena is based why should the parapsychologist be ashamed of following his example? It was in fact due to the collaboration of C. G. Jung with Wolfgang Pauli—one of the greatest physicists of our century—that a speculative theory on these lines was formulated in Jung's essay 'Synchronicity: An Acausal Connecting Principle'. It attempts to ascribe not only the phenomena of parapsychology, but also meaningful coincidences, to the operation of acausal forces in the universe, 'equal in rank to causality as a principle of explanation'. This is not the place to discuss Jung's and other theories on similar lines, which I have written about elsewhere, while the present volume was in press (Koestler 1972; Hardy, Harvie and Koestler 1973).

If, however, the parapsychologist were willing to acknowledge the acausal nature of the psi phenomena, this would imply abandoning the wish-dream of the completely repeatable and predicatable experiment. No two successive photographs of the quantum events photographed in the bubble chamber will ever be exactly alike—only the overall outcome of a great number of unpredictable physical events is predictable by the laws of probability. *Mutatis mutandis,* parapsychology will have to continue to rely mainly on statistical evidence—on the 'weak violations', to borrow Schmidt's term between psi effects and the laws of probability. Such statistical proofs are intuitively less convincing to the non-mathematically minded than precognitive dreams or poltergeist phenomena. But poltergeists are notoriously undisciplined entities, and as unpredictable in their behaviour as the nucleus of a Strontium 90 atom. Thus both the physicist and the parapsychologist are learning to live in a universe with a substructure of non-causal interactions—a fuzzy world of wavering contours, replete with little bubbles of indeterminacy, which provide intimations of an unexpected kind of freedom, for which in the world of classical physics there was no room. Once this lesson has sunk in, 'nothing in science or philosophy could ever again be quite the same', to quote Beloff's introduction. The matter-of-fact, experimental approach of this volume, combined with some tantalising speculations, seems to me a valuable step towards that goal.

## REFERENCES

Cole, J., in *Control of the Mind*, ed. Farber, S. M., and Wilson, R. H. L., New York, 1961.
Hardy, Sir A., Harvie, R., and Koestler, A., *The Challenge of Chance,* Hutchinson, London, 1973.
Koestler, A., *The Roots of Coincidence,* Hutchinson, London, 1972.

# Index